Aston Martin
DB2 • DB3 • DB4 • DB5 • DB6
And the Bertones

ISBN 1 84155 628 9

Text and Photography
by
Colin Pitt

Published by
CP PRESS
www.cppress.co.uk

First published 2007

Acknowledgements

We wish to extend our sincere thanks to Desmond J. Smail, Richard Stewart Williams, Nicholas Mee, Adrian Hamilton and their companies for allowing us to photograph their truly superb collection of cars.

Other Titles
by CP Press

Abarth Sports Racers

Aston Martin Zagato In Perspective

Bentley Continental In Perspective

Ferrari 308 328 348 Enthusiasts Guide

Jensen Interceptor In Perspective

Lotus Book Type 1 to Type 72

Porsche 911RS 911RSR 964RS

Porsche 928 In Perspective

Table of Contents

Aston Martin – The Key Players

Lionel Martin

Lionel Walker Birch Martin was born on 15th March 1878 and was the son of E.M. Martin and his wife.

Robert Bamford and Lionel Martin joined forces to run a motor business in Callow Street, Fulham Road in 1913. They bought and sold small cars of the time such as G.W.K., Calthorpe and Singer. The firm did not stay at Callow Street very long for Hesse & Savory allowed them to take over premises at Henniker Place, South Kensington. Jack Addis was to join them as Works Foreman at Henniker Place while Robert Bamford was Manager.

In competitions of the day Lionel Martin had many successes with a modified and tuned Singer. This lead to requests from customers for similar modifications to their cars.

The First World War saw Lionel Martin selling off all the machinery at Henniker Place, South Kensington to the Sopwith Aviation Company in Kingston, Surrey.

The first priority after the war was to get back together all those who had formed Bamford & Martin Ltd. Before the war and in January 1920 they moved from Henniker Place, South Kensington to 53 Abingdon Road, Kensington. The first prototype was registered AM4656 and was described in The Motor in November 1919.

Lionel Martin, his second wife Katherine and their young son John moved to "The Hollies", 1 Pembroke Villas, Kensington to be nearer to the Abingdon Road works of Bamford & Martin Ltd. Lionel Martin had always appreciated that in order to sell his new products he had to bring the name of Aston Martin to the forefront of the competition events, particularly those such as Brooklands. Lionel Martin's 'final' prototype (AM270) won the Essex Short Handicap at Brooklands in May 1921 with himself driving. In the Le Mans of September 1921 B.S. Marchall gained sixth place in his Aston Martin, "Bunny". Others who competed with Aston Martin cars included Victor Bruce who drove "Coal

Scuttle" and Kensington Moir and Count 'Lou' Zborowski.

In 1924 Aston Martin saw 26 cars leaving the Kensington works for customers while new additional Aston Martin drivers for 1924 included H.S. Eaton and Victor Gillow.

Also in May 1924 John Roby Benson joined the Bamford & Martin Company. Benson was keen to develop a new engine for the Aston Martin.

By mid-1924 Bamford & Martin Ltd. Were in Lionel Martin's debt to some £31,000 and consequently his resources were stretched. John Benson suggested Lionel Martin approach Benson's mother Lady Charnwood and she put up £10,000 and acquired the assets of the old company. In July 1924 a new company was formed with Lionel Martin, Katherine Martin, George Eustace Ridley Shield and John Roby Benson as directors.

Among those continuing to use Aston Martins in competition were Captain Douglas at the wheel of "Razorblade" and Miss Pink who drove "AM270" at Shelsley Walsh.

On 11th November 1925, 53 Abingdon Road became the subject of having the Receiver appointed. Two days after the appointment of the Receiver (Arthur Whale), Lionel Martin found his services dispensed with and he left the works for the last time and a large part of his personal fortune lay beyond recovery.

John Roby Benson made critical remarks in the hearing of others and these got back to Lionel Martin. With having just been dismissed by the Receiver, Lionel Martin would not let such remarks go unnoticed. In fact, Lionel Martin would quickly resort to the processes of law. Benson was alleged to have said that Lionel Martin had been party with Jack Addis in removing Aston Martin working drawings without Benson's knowledge and that Lionel Martin had removed spare parts from the company at the time it was in the Receiver's hands. These were the more serious of the accusations. Lionel Martin became the plaintiff in a slander action against John Roby Benson, the defendant. Lionel Martin was represented by Sir Leslie Scott, KC. The plaintiff, Lionel Martin sued the defendant, John Roby Benson for three separate slanders alleged to have been spoken on the 18th November 1925, the 24th November 1925 and the 27th November 1925. The words complained of contained a number of serious allegations against the plaintiff and they accused the plaintiff of three felonies – larceny, criminal conspiracy and dishonesty. John Roby Benson pleaded non-publication and justification. After a trial lasting many days the jury found that the defendant had in fact published the words complained of and that as to each separate matter of justification that the plea of justification had not been proved by the defendant.

However, upon seven separate heads the jury dealt with they awarded a total of 1 ¾ d damages. Lionel Martin claimed that the Aston Martin working drawings had been removed to the company's solicitors for the benefit of anyone interested in the rescue of the company and denied being a party with Addis or anyone else in placing cast-iron bolts in the Benson engine.

But in addition to being awarded just 1 ¾ d damages,

McCardie J. also refused to award Lionel Martin his costs.

"Recognizing as I do that each case must depend on its own particular facts, I am satisfied in the present action that I ought to make an order depriving the plaintiff of costs. I have no doubt that the verdict of the jury meant, either that the statements made were so nearly true that ignominious damages would suffice, or that the plaintiff's character was so bad that contemptuous damages should be given. This I think is the basic explanation of the assessment by the jury, after the fullest deliberation, of one farthing damages only upon each head of claim, including the charges of felony. Nor do I doubt that the jury took the view that in any event the conduct of the plaintiff had been open to the gravest suspicion, that it called for severe condemnation, and that the plaintiff had brought the defamation upon himself. In my opinion the jury were amply warranted, upon the circumstances revealed at the trial, in assessing the damages at the smallest sum that could be given.

I make an order depriving the plaintiff of costs.

Lionel Martin moved to The Hollies, 1 Pembroke Villas, Kensington, to be nearer 53 Abingdon Road, which was just a short walk away

The judgement will be entered for 1¾ d without costs."

Eventually, John Roby Benson's parents (the Charnwoods) purchased the goodwill and assets of the old company and approached the Birmingham firm of Renwick and Bertelli with a view to amalgamating.

On 12th October 1926 the firm of Aston Martin Motors Ltd. was incorporated and a new chapter was about to begin.

After the collapse of the company in 1925 Lionel Martin and his family continued to live at "The Hollies", Pembroke Villas, Kensington, but in 1932 they moved to "Palings", Warboys Road, Kingston-on-Thames, Surrey.

William Sommerville Renwick and Lord Charnwood owned equal parts of the new company Aston Martin Motors Ltd. Renwick had worked for Armstrong Siddeley at Coventry. It was there that he had met Augustus Cesare "Bert" Bertelli who was to design production Aston Martins of the period 1926 to 1937.

Benson and Lord Charnwood departed and in 1928 the firm was reconstructed as Aston Martin Limited. The Chairman was to be S.C. Whitehead and in 1931 Renwick left to go to America.

With the exception of the years 1929, 1930 and 1934, Aston Martin ran cars at Le Mans every year from 1928 to 1964. In 1935 Aston Martin achieved third place at Le Mans.

In 1932, Sir Arthur Munro Sutherland bought Aston Martin for his son Robert Gordon Sutherland to manage. He was to share joint managing directorship of the company with Bert Bertelli.

Bertelli and Sutherland had disagreements over what Bertelli believed was a dilution of the company's sporting pedigree. Bertelli departed from Feltham in 1937 and his assistant Claude Hill took over design.

Sir David Brown

David Brown was an apprentice who started work in 1921 at the age of 17 in a gear manufacturing works founded by his grandfather in 1860. He was not particularly keen about gears and gear-manufacturing at the beginning and would have preferred to have started off in the automobile industry, but he eventually found the art of gear-making quite fascinating and began to thoroughly enjoy work in the Huddersfield plant.

During the first year of his apprenticeship he also found time to build the inevitable "special" using a chassis of his own design and a 2-litre Sage engine. Later, when Amherst Villiers, known as a formidable tuner of motor cars, arrived in Huddersfield to ask Messrs David Brown and Sons Ltd. If they would car to build a new super-charger which was to be fitted on the Raymond Mays Vauxhall Special, David brown – now foreman in the worm-gear department – took an immediate interest in the project. At this time the David Brown Company was already making various components for motor car manufacturers.

In 1860 the David Brown organisation occupied only a small workshop and had a staff of exactly two. In 1910 the company was already considered the largest gear-making firm in the British Commonwealth and when war started in 1914, they had established a large plant in Huddersfield.

Expansion continued after the First World War and soon two old-established engineering firms, the Keighley Gear Company and P.R. Jackson Ltd. Were acquired and incorporated in the parent organisation.

It was a strange coincidence that David Brown, as foreman of the worm gear department, was responsible for the manufacture of rear axle components which were fitted in a new car designed by A.C. Bertelli and announced on the eve of the 1927 Olympia Motor Show as the Aston Martin – "the car that is built for the owner's pleasure."

David Brown and Sons built the supercharger for the Vauxhall Villiers, a car David brown later drove in circuit and sprint events. The David Brown Company also went on to manufacture superchargers for the production 4 ½ litre "blower" Bentley cars and for the Tim Birkin-Doroth Paget racing team.

In 1926 David Brown's apprenticeship ended. He was then promoted to foreman in the worm gear department at Huddersfield. In 1927 he progressed to the appointment of assistant works manager and in 1928 became manager of the Keighley gear department. In 1929 he was elected to the board of David Brown and Sons Ltd. And in 1932 became managing director at the age of 28. In later years some of his co-directors were to oppose some of his proposals and could equally have opposed his appointment as managing director at the very beginning if this had been thought necessary.

David Brown developed a new tractor of his own and it was produced in time for the Royal Show in 1939. A separate manufacturing company, David Brown Tractors Ltd. Was then formed and housed in a converted cotton mill at Meltham near Huddersfield. Before the end of the second world war, David Brown further enhanced group productive capacity by acquiring three more companies, Muir Machine Tools Ltd., David Brown Gears (London) Ltd. and the Coventry Gear Company. In 1945 he established the David Brown Tool Company.

In October 1959 at a dinner in Park Lane, London, David Brown stated that;

"I have often been asked, since winning the Sports Car Championship, 'What are your future plans?'

In answering this, I think it necessary to go back to our early days of racing, some ten years ago, when we were competing with more or less standard DB2 saloons. And to remind you just how standard these cars were, I used one of the team cars, VMF 64, for my own personal transport in between its racing appearances.

The whole character of racing has, however, changed, until today an ordinary production car would stand about as much chance in a race as the proverbial snowball of getting into hell! The sports-racing car of today has become a more complicated and expensive version of a Grand Prix car, with the addition of a self-starter, lighting, mudguards, two seats, windscreen, etc.

To remain in the hunt today it is necessary to design, build and develop completely new cars every few years.

This leads to the big question: what is the purpose of sports car racing? – and it seems to me that it has departed very much from the original intention when sports car racing first started. I would like to see sports car racing where the cars are closely allied to what the public can buy.

For Grand Prix racing, on the other hand, the problem should be of producing within a prescribed formula the fastest machine that is possible, regardless of other constraints. Both forms of racing serve a useful purpose but they should be complementary to one another and not merely variations on a theme.

I believe that sports car racing has reached an important cross-roads – and nobody appears sure which way to go. The regulations for Le Mans – only seven months away – are still unknowns and the formula laid down in 1958 for World Championships, which was to run for three years, has already, before its third year, been altered. Even the DBR1 on our stand [at the London Motor Show] is not eligible in its present form to race next year.

Furthermore, we have been racing continuously for something over ten years and during that period our production has remained fairly static. On the other hand we have developed, as a result of racing, a very fine product which seems to be very much in demand. We feel it is now time we devoted a greater part of our efforts to this commercial aspect of our business and a greater part of our technical resources to the more rapid development of our production cars.

I have strong views on what the future of sports car racing should be and it is with regret that I have to tell you that we do not intend to compete in sports car racing next year. Our own racing efforts in 1960 will be concentrated upon the Grand Prix field in this last year of the present Grand Prix Formula.

I should like to think that if, and when, we return to sports car racing, it will be something that more closely resembles our production car and what the public can buy."

David Brown visited the Feltham factory, tried the Atom saloon and bought the company with Claude Hill and Gordon Sutherland remaining.

Alan Good of Lagonda launched the LB6 in 1945 calling it the Lagonda – Bentley. A lawsuit with Rolls followed which Lagonda lost and Alan Good put Lagonda up for sale.

David Brown learnt that Rootes and Jaguar were interested in Lagonda but were deterred by the economic outlook. David brown eventually bought the company, though not its premises, for £52,000.

Initially Aston Martin DB2/4 bodies were built by Mulliners and the Lagondas went to Tickford, Newport Pagnell. Tickford became part of the David Brown empire in 1955 and DB2/4 bodies then went there. For David Brown the best way of promoting the road cars and proving their components was to go racing. This affected much of his thinking and of those he employed.

At the same time that Aston Martin was sold to Company Developments (1972), so the tractor division was sold to Tenneco. David Brown died in 1993.

Harold Beach

Born in 1913, Harold Beach started his working life as an apprentice at the coachbuilding firm Barkers, who made Rolls-Royce bodies. After that he took a job with William Beardmore (builders of commercial vehicles) as a draughtsman at their Earlsfield factory. Then Harold Beach spent a period with another ex-Barkers employee, James Ridlington. As the war approached there was another job change for Harold Beach, this time with the Hungarian engineer Straussler at his Park Royal factory as a designer working on airfield components.

In 1950, Harold Beach saw an advert for a design draughtsman for David Brown Tractors (Engineering) Automobile Division at Feltham. After an interview with the chief draughtsman, Frank Ayto, Harold Beach started in September 1950.

Harold Beach started work on a successor to the Aston Martin DB2 at the time Eberan von Eberhorst was made chief engineer. Von Eberhorst had been with Auto-Union before the war. But

Harold Beach was to find that Eberan von Eberhorst had different ideas to him and scrapped all the work they had done on a DB2 successor.

Harold Beach was involved with work on a replacement for the Aston Martin DB2/4 and this was called Project 114. But once again his plans were to be thrown into disarray. John Wyer, who had been appointed competitions manager in 1950, was made general manager in 1956. Wyer had the idea that they should go to Touring of Milan for them to style a body on Harold Beach's perimeter frame. They turned round and said they did not want to build on Beach's design but wanted a platform frame instead. Beach's front and rear suspension of Project 114 were however retained. Harold Beach's proposed perimeter frame regarded the chassis as separate from the body, while Touring of Milan's platform frame regarded the chassis and body as almost one.

The "Superleggera" principle involves a strong platform chassis and a steel framework onto which the body panels are fixed. Components such as wheel arches are thereby part of the chassis and not added afterwards gaining greater stiffness.

Harold Beach also worked closely with Tadek Marek on the redesign of the 2.9 litre engine.

The Aston Martin DBS was introduced in 1967 and Harold Beach was responsible for its chassis and suspension. And it featured a de Dion rear axle that Harold Beach had proposed on a production model ten years earlier.

In 1972, David Brown, who had owned Aston Martin since Harold Beach joined them 22 years previously, sold the company to a property company called Company Developments. They decided to keep Harold Beach on.

In 1973 the chairman, William Willson, made Harold Beach director of engineering.

From June 1975, Harold Beach continued to work with the new owners Peter Sprague and George Minden, though no longer as a director.

Harold Beach retired in 1978, having served under three ownerships.

Tadek Marek

Tadek Marek was born in Krakow, Poland in 1908. He graduated from Charlottenburg Technical Institute in Berlin with a diploma in engineering.

After the war Tadek and his wife Peggy went to Germany for a short period but returned again to Britain.

In 1948 he got a job with the Austin Motor Corporation at Longbridge.

He left Austin and despite a job offer with Holden Motors in Australia, went to Aston Martin. It was probably Feltham general manager James Stirling who was responsible for bringing Tadek Marek to Aston Martin.

The 1950's saw many significant Aston Martin characters coming and going. In 1950, Harold Beach, John Wyer and Robert Eberan von Eberhorst joined the development team. Others who joined included stylist Frank Feeley, chief draughtsman Frank Ayto and designer Willy Watson.

Among those who left Aston Martin were Gordon Sutherland, Jock St. John Horsfall and Claude Hill.

When Tadek Marek had finished his apprenticeship under Harold Beach he made improvements to the old 2.9 engine which was a temporary measure until the introduction of an all-new unit.

The "new" 2.9 litre engine was first seen in the DB Mark III that was introduced in March 1957 and although the cubic capacity remained the same it had a new block, new crankcase and new oil pump.

Tadek's redesign of the 2.9 engine showed his talent for this sort of work and gave Aston Martin breathing space until work could begin on an all-new engine for the all-new Aston Martin DB4.

What shortcomings that remained in Tadek Marek's 3.7 litre engine for the Aston Martin DB4 were finally put right in the 4.0 litre engine that was fitted to the Aston Martin DB5 in July 1963.

In the early 1960's John Wyer decided work should commence on a new engine to power the next generation of Aston Martins and concluded a V8 configuration would be best. Tadek began work on designing this engine in 1963. As it came from the drawing board the unit was a 4.8 litre capable of developing 324 bhp with four vertical twin choke carburettors.

Tadek Marek did all the engine design drawings himself and he had a man in the design department working for him called Alan Crouch who did all the design and layout work.

Victor Gauntlett

Born in 1942, Victor Gauntlett made much of his money from the petrochemicals industry.

In 1980, Victor Gauntlett put £500,000 into Aston Martin Lagonda which amounted to a ten per cent stake. In 1981 he became executive chairman at a time when Aston Martin were producing four cars a week. It was Victor Gauntlett who, in the 1980's, renewed the association with Zagato and Aston Martin sold fifty-two Vantage Zagato couples which cost £86,000 each.

Prior to coming to Aston Martin he had founded and sold Pace Petroleum and in 1988 he founded Proteus Petroleum. He died in 2003, aged 60

Alan Curtis

Alan Curtis had been interested in Aston Martin in 1975 and had been prepared to pay £650,000 for the company. But he learned it had been bought by a consortium comprising Peter Sprague (an American) and George Minden (a Canadian). But the Englishman of the consortium was no longer involved and Peter Sprague called Alan Curtis saying he had heard that he was interested in saving the company and that without an Englishman he (Peter Sprague) would not continue.

So in 1975, Aston Martin Lagonda's quartet of shareholders were Peter Sprague, George Minden, Alan Curtis and a retired steel businessman Denis Flather.

At the end of 1975, Alan Curtis along with Denis Flather became directors of Aston Martin. In March 1977, Alan Curtis became managing director of Aston Martin.

Four members of the senior management were made associate directors and these were Mike Loasby (director of engineering), David Flink (director of manufacturing), Nigel Butten (director of finance) and Tony Nugent (director of sales).

Rex Woodgate

Rex Woodgate was born in 1926 and had a job as an equipment tester at British Acoustic Films. Then he got a job with Thomson and Taylor who built racing and record breaking cars at Brooklands. He worked as a mechanic to Stirling Moss, preparing his car for the 1949 season, before joining H.W. Motors of Walton-on-Thames as a mechanic until 1950. Reg Parnell recommended Rex Woodgate to John Wyer and he was engaged to build production versions of the Aston Martin DB3S in 1954.

Rex Woodgate also worked on the DB3S's replacement the DBR1 and then the DBR2.

In the middle of 1961, Rex Woodgate rejoined Aston Martin and was factory service representative for North America. Rex Woodgate was convinced that Aston Martin should set up its own importership rather than using several importers and distributors. In May 1964,

Aston Martin Lagonda Incorporated was opened near Philadelphia and it stayed there for fourteen years.

In 1971, Rex Woodgate was made President of Aston Martin Lagonda Incorporated.

John Wyer

John Wyer was made Competitions Manager at Aston Martin in 1950 and was made General manager in 1956. Reg Parnell succeeded him as Competitions Manager.

John Wyer had been pit manager of Dudley Folland's privately entered pre-war Aston Martin. Upon retirement he went to live in Arizona and he died in 1989.

William Towns

In 1936 William Towns was born, fairly near to Guildford. In 1955 William Towns joined the Rootes Company and found that there was a department within the Rootes Company that did in full size what he had done as a lad with plasticine. The person in charge of Rootes' styling studio at the time was Ted White. Ted White as the department Head of Styling was more an administrator than stylist because management (seven members of the Rootes family) were the stylists and the supposed stylists were more akin to modellers for the management.

William Towns stayed with Rootes for eight years before moving to Rover for more money and at a time the Rover 2000 was being developed. William Lyons, upon seeing the full-scale wooden mock-up of the Rover 2000, thought that its styling was abysmal and that it was badly proportioned. But Towns thought that the interior was excellent.

While at Rover, William Towns worked on three projects. The first involved working on proposals for a Targa-topped two plus two sports car based on the Rover 2000 saloon. Sketches were made but nothing came of them. William Towns next project concerned the gas turbine racer that was developed for Le Mans. For the 1963 Le Mans the gas turbine racer was entered as an open roadster. But for the 1965 Le Mans, William Towns was to develop a closed body version of the gas turbine racer. Towns produced a scale model which was subsequently wind tunnel tested before being made into a full-size body. The third project was a car intended for the film world. William Towns drew up a very low sports, based again on the Rover 2000 platform. Although a quarter-scale model was made nothing came of it once again.

William Towns had been at Rover three years when somebody mentioned that there was a job going at Aston Martin. But Aston Martin did not have a styling job on offer, they had openings for a body engineer and for a seat designer. William Towns went to them and they offered him a job designing seats at first.

Later, Harold Beach told William Towns they wanted to do a four door car. Towns explained that you have to design the four door version first and then shorten it if you wish to make a two door. William Towns was later asked to produce scale models of his proposals and he created a two door and a four door side by side. The latter became the Lagonda model of 1974.

In 1969 William Towns was offered the job of Chief Stylist at Triumph but he preferred to work for them on a freelance basis. Replacements for the Triumph 1300 and 2000 saloons (code-named Puma and Bobcat) were cars that Towns was brought in to work on.

Aston Martin kept in touch with William Towns and when the 6-cylinder Aston Martin DBS became the V8 he produced the styling. However, proposals for gull-winged versions of an Aston Martin and Lagonda came to nothing.

Augustus Bertelli

Many regard Augustus Bertelli as the father of Aston Martin. Bertelli was born in the Italian town of Genoa in 1890; he and his family moved to Cardiff in 1894. On leaving school he took up a general engineering apprenticeship in Cardiff. He then, took a job with Fiat in Turin. Bertelli was riding mechanic to Felice Nazzaro in a Fiat for the Coppa Florio. Grahame-Whites, manufacturers of French aircraft, took Bertelli on to develop an engine of his.

Augustus Cesare Bertelli married Vera in 1918 at Hendon, and they moved to Golders Green. Bertelli was given a job at Birmingham-based Alldays and Onions and he designed a new Enfield-Alldays car.

In 1924, Bertelli and W.S. Renwick teamed up in business in Birmingham. Renwick and Bertelli bought Aston Martin from John Benson and kept him on. Really, John Benson had nothing but the goodwill of Aston Martin. Augustus Bertelli and W.S. Renwick then moved to Feltham and they then took on Claude Hill. Within a year of starting at Feltham, they had produced a completely new Aston Martin with a 1 ½ litre engine. The end of the 1920s and the start of the 1930s saw the Aston Martin name carried on the 1 ½ litre series and had names such as International, Ulster and Le Mans.

Augustus Bertelli's brother, Enrico Bertelli, ran a coach-building business next to the Aston Martin factory at Feltham, hence the beautiful bodies of the early Aston Martin cars in an era of genuine hand-built cars.

Benson and Renwick eventually left the company and Claude Hill left twice, once in 1928 and once in 1934. In 1936, Bertelli left and the company was in the control of the Sutherland family at a time when the 2-litre cars were being introduced.

Just before World War II, Bertelli took a job with a firm called High Duty Alloys, where he stayed until 1955.

Dr. Ulrich Bez

Dr. Ulrich Bez has become the new Chief Executive of Aston Martin in 2000, having had twenty-eight years in the Motor Industry. He has previously been responsible for product design and development at Porsche, BMW and Daewoo.

Dr. Ulrich Bez was born in November 1943 in Bad Cannstatt, Germany and has a Doctorate in Engineering from the University of Stuttgart. He takes over from Bob Dover, who is to remain on Aston Martin's Board of Directors.

The Homes of Aston Martin

Next to 53 Abingdon Road is Vantage Place. Few of the locals realise its significance

However, on the wall of Vantage Place is this sign showing it was formerly the works of the makers of Aston Martin.

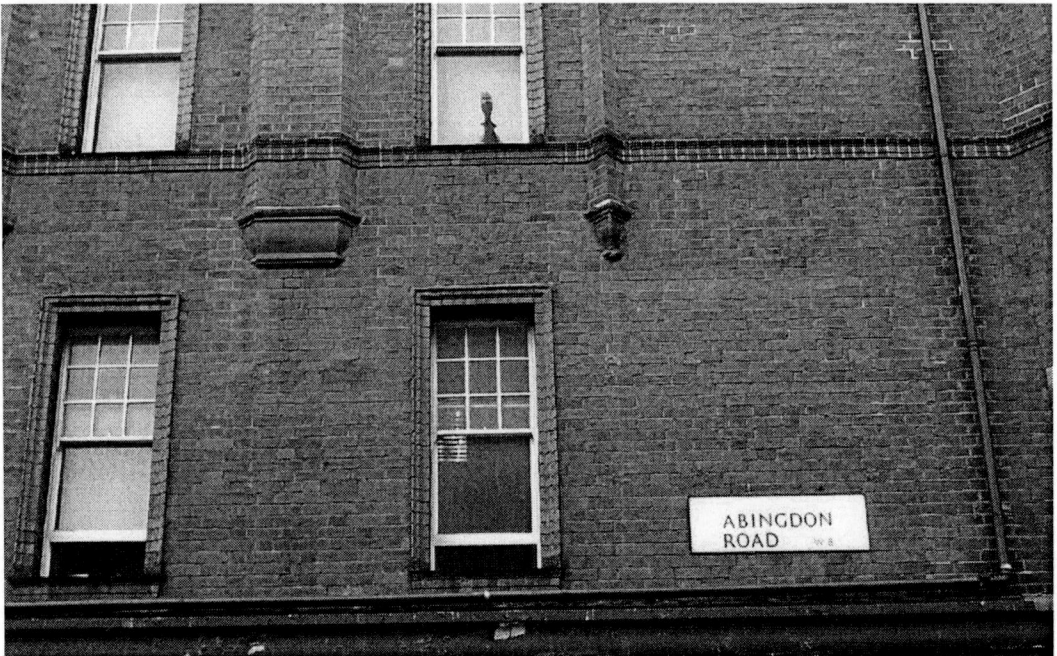

53 Abingdon Road, just off High Street Kensington

The Homes of Aston Martin

Victoria Road, Feltham was the next home of Aston Martin

Aston Martin's current home in Tickford Street, Newport Pagnell

Its current premises are on both sides of the road in Tickford Street. Flags are flying above one of its many buildings.

Aston Works, Newport Pagnell

Aston Martin DB2

The chassis of the Aston Martin DB2 was similar to that of the Aston Martin DB1 but the wheelbase was only 8 feet 3 inches. Frank Feeley designed the two-seater body.

Some of the first cars constructed (chassis LMA/49/1 and chassis LMA/49/2) had the four cylinder 1980 cc engines, while chassis LML/49/3 had a Lagonda six-cylinder engine.

In the first post-war Le Mans 24 Hours, the Aston Martin DB2 cars were driven by A. Jones and N. Haines, T.A.S.O. Mathieson and P. Maréchal, and L. Johnson and C. Brackenbury. It was not a good race for Aston Martin as LML/49/3 retired after 6 laps and LMA/49/1 was crashed by Pierre Maréchal and he died the following day from his injuries. The Aston Martin DB2 of Jones and Haines gained 7th place. The Aston Martin DB2 cars (chassis numbers LMA/49/1, LMA/49/2 and LML/49/3) were registered with the registration numbers UMC 64, UMC 65 and UMC 66 respectively. LMA/49/1 and LMA/49/3 were entered for the Spa 24 Hours race of 1949. At the Le Mans 24 Hours of 1949

a total of six Aston Martin cars had been entered and the other three were a private production Aston Martin DB1 and two 1936 Aston Martin Speed Models.

At the Belgian 24 Hours at Spa, Johnson and Brackenbury finished 3rd overall in the Aston Martin LMA/49/3 (UMC 66) whilst N. Haines and L. Macklin in the Aston Martin LMA/49/1 (UMC 64), now rebuilt, came 5th overall. Lance Macklin had driven a Bentley 8 litre at Le Mans the previous year.

St. J. Horsfall, driving an Aston Martin Speed Model (J6/707/U) came 4th overall at the 1949 Spa 24 Hours and was driving solo.

In 1950, the Aston Martin DB2 was put into production and also John Wyer was to run the works team. A 1949 Aston Martin DB2 (LML/49/4) which had been used for development purposes was now made available. A drop-head Aston Martin DB2 was added to the range by the time of the London Motor Show of 1950.

In standard form the Aston Martin DB2 of 1950 had a 6.5 to 1 compression ratio

Aston Martin DB2

and had twin SU H4 carburettors delivering 105 bhp at 5,000 rpm. In January 1951 a "Vantage" option boosted output to 125 bhp with a compression ratio of 8.16 to 1 and had larger SU HV6 carburettors.

Lance Macklin went to Monza for the Coppa Inter Europe using the development car LML/49/4 (UMC 272) and finished fourth overall.

For the Le Mans 24 Hours of 1950 Wyer prepared three cars; LML/50/7 (registered VMF 63), LML/50/8 (registered VMF 64) and LML/50/9 (registered VMF 65). These cars were the first three production cars, and all had the LB6E 2.6 litre engine. Macklin, Brackenbury, Abecassis, Fairman, Parnell and Thompson were signed up as drivers. Jack Fairman crashed VMF 65 (LML/50/9) putting himself in hospital and the car out of the race. LML/49/3 (UMC 66) had been taken to Le Mans as a spare car and this was quickly race prepared fro John Gordon to replace Jack Fairman, and partnering Eric Thompson. But UMC 66 (LML/49/3) retired from the race with a broken crankshaft after eight laps.

Directors of H.W. Motors, George Abecassis, and Macklin in the Aston Martin DB2, chassis number LML/50/8 (VMF 64), finished 5th overall. Brackenbury and Parnell in the Aston Martin DB2, chassis number LML/50/7 (VMF 63) came 6th overall. LML/50/8 (VMF 64) set a new Class D distance record. George Abecassis had stated that the Aston Martin DB2s with a maximum speed just over 120 mph meant they were left behind by Jaguar XK1210s and never even saw Ferraris and Talbots. But they made up ground with good brakes, good handling and good reliability.

This race marked the first appearance of Reg Parnell in the Aston Martin team. On the 20th August Parnell (VMF 63), Macklin (VMF 64) and Thompson (VMF 65) were entered in the One Hour Production Car Race at the International Trophy meeting, Silverstone. Macklin's place was taken by Raymond Sommer. The Aston Martin drivers finished 10th (Sommer in LML/50/8), 12th (Parnell in LML/50/7) and 15th (Thompson in LML/50/9) at Silverstone in August 1950.

At the Tourist Trophy (Dunrod circuit) in Northern Ireland on 16th September, the Aston Martin DB2s were not fast enough; Stirling Moss with Tom Wisdom's Jaguar XK120 was the winner. Reg Parnell in LML/50/7 was 4th, G. Abecassis in LML/50/9 was 5th and L. Macklin in LML/50/8 was 7th overall.

For 1951, Wyer built two lightweight Aston Martin DB2s, LML/50/50 (XMC 76) and LML/50/55 (XMC 77). This was despite opposition from von Eberhorst. The cars were 450 lb lighter and had 18-gauge alloy instead of 16-gauge. In the Mille Miglia, Tom Wisdom partnered by Tony Hume, drove LML/50/8 (VMF 64) to 11th place overall at 68.79 mph and won the class for closed cars and convertibles over 2,000 cc.

The two new Aston Martin DB2 lightweights made their first appearance at the Daily Express Silverstone meeting. Abecassis in LML/50/55 (XMC 77) retired with a seized gearbox. Parnell finished 7th with LML/50/50 (XMC 76) and won the 3-litre class. Wyer only built two lightweight Aston Martin DB2s as he believed that at least one

Aston Martin DB3 would be ready for Le Mans but this was not the case. So Aston Martin entered the two lightweight Aston Martin DB2s as well as LML/50/8. All cars now had aluminium cylinder heads, three Weber twin-choke 35DCO carburettors and developed 138 bhp. Two private Aston Martin DB2s were also entered at Le Mans.

The Jaguar C-Type of Peter Walker and Peter Whitehead won Le Mans 1951. But Lance Macklin and Eric Thompson in LML/50/8 were 3rd overall (4th in the Index of Performance) whilst George Abecassis and Brian Shawe-Taylor were 5th overall in LML/50/50 (XMC 77) and Reg Parnell and David Hampshire were 7th overall in XMC 76. The privately entered cars of Nigel Mann and Mortimer Morris Goodall (LML/50/59) and Peter Clark and Jack Scott (LML/50/57) were 19th and 22nd overall, respectively.

At the Tourist Trophy on 15th September 1951 Brian Shawe-Taylor drove the Aston Martin DB2 (LML/50/50 reg. no. XMC 76) in 7th place overall while Eric Thompson drove the Aston Martin DB2 LML/50/9 in

8th place overall (and 3rd in its class).

In 1952 Eric Thompson in the Aston Martin DB2 (XMC 76) and Dennis Poore in the Aston Martin DB2 (XMC 77) were 1st and 3rd respectively in the Goodwood Easter Handicap. In the 1952 Mille Miglia, Abecassis in Aston Martin DB2 LML/50/55 retired with clutch problems. But Tom Wisdom partnered by Hume finished 12th overall in Aston Martin DB2 LML/50/8.

At the 18th May 1952 Prix de Berne, Geoff Duke came fourth in the Aston Martin DB2 LML/50/55. At Le Mans 1952 the privately entered Aston Martin DB2 of Peter Clark/Mike Keen (LML/50/57) came 7th overall.

In 1955 Aston Martin entered a full team of Aston Martin DB2 14s in the Monte Carlo Rally. By August 1954 the 2,580 cc engine had been replaced by the 2,922 cc unit.

54 DMF (LML/857), 55 DMF (LML/784) and 56 DMF (LML/855) were the Monte Carlo Rally cars.

Maurice Gatsonides and Marcel Becquart in 55 DMF were 7th overall and won their class. Peter Collins and Graham Whitehead finished 95th.

In the 1956 RAC British Rally, the Aston Martin DB2 of Lyndon Sims and J. Ambrose (LML/50/X2) was victorious.

For the 1958 Sebring 12 Hours race an Aston Martin DB2 MK III (AM 300/3/1312) was driven by George Constantine and John Dalton in the GT category but it retired with hub failure.

The Privateers with Aston Martin DB2

Privately-entered DB2s began to appear in competition during the 1951 season. The first race appearance of the car in private hands came at the Nottingham SCC's Gamston meeting in March when Peter Reece's early drophead model (LML/50/34) finished 2nd in a handicap ahead of Ben Whitehouse who had purchased UMC 65, still with 1,970 cc engine. Another ex-team car reappeared when Rob Walker took over VMF 65. George Abecassis drove the car to 11th place in the British Empire Trophy for its new owner after "it boiled like a tea kettle", while Eric Thompson later took 8th place and 3rd in class with the car in the TT. Tony Rolt, Walker's principal driver in the ERA-Delage at the time, also drove the car, but VMF 65 was used most extensively, and successfully, by the owner in sprint events. In 1953 its engine was replaced by a 2,922 cc DB3 unit and in this form the car was tested again by John Bolster in Autosport. The more powerful engine certainly made a difference to the performance figures on a car over which Bolster still enthused. The maximum speed had gone up to 131.5 mph, while the acceleration figures for 0-50 and 0-100 mph tumbled to 7.2 and 21 seconds respectively.

For Le mans in 1951 two private DB2s joined the team cars, those of Nigel Mann (PPJ 2, LML/50/59) and Peter Clark (MKC 306, LML/50/57). These were genuine "off the shelf" production cars fitted with long-range tanks and hard linings. The then AMOC president. Mortimer Morris-Goodall drove with Mann and their 10th place was backed up by Clark and Jack Scott in 13th place. According to Nigel Mann, "Mort Morris-Goodall and I had a very nice ride!". Clark also finished 10th in the TT that year. The following year the same two cars again ran at Le Mans and although the Mann/Morris-Goodall car retired with a flat battery after the dynamo bracket broke at an ungodly 4am, the two-way radio equipped Clark/Michael Keen version, which now ran with four SU carburettors, finished 7th overall, 3rd in class, and 4th in the Rudge Whitworth Biennial Cup, thereby saving face for Astons' (not for the last time by a private owner at Le Mans) after the elimination of the works entries. The innovative Clark later ran MKC 306 with a Wade supercharger, without conspicuous success. Just one DB2/4 ran at Le mans, the 2.9 DB3-engined version of Hernano da Silva Ramos/J.P. Colas which, in 1954, became the last Feltham saloon to race in the French classic. The car ran a differential bearing and dropped out in what was a dreadful race for Astons. Da Silva Ramos, who later drove for the Gordini Grand Prix team, did have several successes at Montlery and finished 16th overall in the 1955 Mille Miglia with his Aston.

DB2s became more numerous in club events from 1952 and at the same time started appearing in lesser foreign competitions – in France, Portugal and Canada in particular. Notably successful were: Tony Everard with AY 2 (LML/50/277 – the Aston Martin chassis "calendar" stuck at '50!), the first of a series of much campaigned Astons which later appeared under the delightful banner of The Vermin Stable; and

Captain (later Major) R.L. Woods who ran LML/50/199 with the DB3 engine from VMF 65 (which he also owned ex-Walker) in 1955, and has since repurchased the car which was last raced by Jean Bloxham in 1956. The latter, a deceptively petite driver of considerable agility who went on to greater things with DB3S models, also ran LML/50/243 at one stage, and she was just one of several prominent lady drivers who favoured the well-mannered DB2 and its later derivatives. Patsy Burt and Angela Brown (DB's daughter and now Mrs. George Abecassis) immediately spring to mind.

Although a frequent award winner, the DB2 was in a rather anomalous position in British club competition. Until Autosport inaugurated a national series-production sports car championship in 1956, production sports cars normally had to compete against sports-racing machinery, against which they had little chance of success. Only handicap races, such as those run by the BARC at Goodwood, and later at Aintree and Mallory, gave cars of the DB2's type a chance of winning in sports car racing. However, in the relatively unstructured world of mid '50s club sport, only the BRDC at Silverstone had bothered to formulate thoroughly considered regulations for Saloon or Touring Car racing. Other clubs just lumped together everything with a roof and called the result a Closed Car class. Not surprisingly DB2s and the odd XK120 and XK140 FHC tended to be on top whenever they entered. Only when Rob Walker and Tommy Atkins produced a pair of Mercedes 300SLs did the Astons have worries in the 3-litre class at sprint events! Perhaps more than anywhere else Goodwood was the happy hunting ground of the Feltham cars. The BARC's programmes of mainly handicap racing at their club meetings suited the Astons but the slightly elevated "garden party" tone of these meetings (in sharp contrast to the 500 cc F3 jousts at Brands Hatch Stadium) was one which accorded well with the refined, rather expensive, and unquestionably classy DB2. During these years it was relatively unusual to see one of the pioneer DB1s in competition, but THX 231 (AMC/48/2), the first David

Brown car sold to the public, gained some awards in 1952 Scottish events for owner Ian McDonald, and three years later actually won the AMOC's premier racing event, the St. John Horsfall Trophy, in the hands of John Bekaert, who was later to distinguish himself in much more powerful Jaguar-engined machinery.

The DB2 and DB2/4 did well in several lesser foreign races, particularly when driven by Mike Sparken and da Silva Ramos, but some of the best performances came in rallies. The car's good handling, reliability and comfort, when allied to the not inconsiderable performance made it a good, if expensive, rally car for the classic rallies of the time which were often long, fast and gruelling. There was no allowance for extensive "rebuilding" along the way, but the extremely specialised vehicles of today were not called for. Tommy Wisdom had shown the way with VMF 64 and others soon emulated him.

Sixth place, and 2nd in class, on the International Lisbon Rally in 1952 fell to S.K. Hansen in LML/50/79, which he still owns today. Circuit men Mann/Morris-Goodall achieved

16th and 20th places overall, and 4th and 2nd places in class respectively in successive racing-orientated Tours de France Automobile with PPJ 2 ("which ended up in a telegraph pole in Hyeres – the only time Morris-Goodall wasn't driving with me"), while PUM6 (LML/50/231) took over where VMF 64 left off and, guided by Arnold Burton/Burke, took 7th overall, a Coupe des Alpes and a class win in the '54 Alpine Rally.

A most successful Aston rallying combination was that of Lyndon Sims and a certain Tony Ambrose with NGO 651, a very late model DB2 Saloon (LML/50/X2) which was works maintained. Sims was already a respected and very fast rally driver, particularly associated with Rileys, when NGO 651 came on the scene, and with it he won Astons' one and only outright victory in an FIA European Touring Championship rally. Unfortunately, this was in the 1956 RAC Rally, "The Rally of the Tests", which attracted few foreign entries and even contemporarily seemed very

tame to those with Alpine or Liege experience. Nevertheless, the event was contested by the British works teams and independent experts and proved that the three-year-old Aston was agile as well as fairly powerful. The same combination also finished 10th overall and won its class on that year's Tulip Rally. There was no RAC in 1957, Suez year, but in 1958 Sims/Ambrose/NGO 651 returned and finished runner-up to the works Rapier of Peter Harper/Bill Deane in atrocious weather conditions. In 1959 Sims used a DB2/4, actually the ex-Monte 56 DMF, and with this, and navigated by Rupert Jones, he finished a (for him) lowly 32nd on the RAC.

Two other DB2/4s did particularly well on major rallies, those of Ron Faulkner and Count Charles de Salis. The latter's Mk II version (SXU 562) brought home a third Coupe des Alpes in 1956 (11th overall and 2nd in class), while with his similar TXU 988 he won his class in the Tulip ('58) and the Monte ('59).

The Aston Martin DB2/4 Mark I's leather interior

Instrumentation on the Aston Martin DB2/4 Mark I

Aston Martin DB2

This Aston Martin DB2/4 is chassis number LML/566 and has the registration CSN 888

Engine of the Aston Martin DB2, the engine number is VB6E/60/1297

Aston Martin DB2 Engine

Configuration	Six cylinders in line, overhead valves, twin overhead camshafts
Capacity	2,580 cc
Bore	78 mm
Stroke	90 mm
Compression Ratio	6.5:1 (Vantage: 8.16:1)
Firing Order	1 – 5 – 3 – 6 – 2 – 4
Valve Timing	io 18° atdc
BHP	105 @ 5,000 rpm
Crankshaft – number of bearings	4
Crankshaft – main bearing	63.5 mm diameter
Crankshaft – big end	51 mm diameter
Ignition Timing	5° btdc
Carburettors	Twin 1 ½ inch SU H4
Gearbox - Gear Ratios	3.77, 5.02, 7.48 and 11.03 to 1; reverse 11.03 to 1. Central gearchange: 3.77, 4.75, 7.05 and 11.03 to 1

Dashboard detail of the Aston Martin DB2/4 Mark I

Aston Martin DB2 Chassis

Wheelbase	2515 mm
Track	1372 mm
Length	4128 mm
Width	1651 mm
Weight (dry)	2464 lb
Suspension	Independent at front, live axle at rear, coil springs all round
Wheels and Tyres	Dunlop centre-lock wires, 5.75 or 6.00 x 16 in.
Brakes	Girling 2LS hydraulic, drums 12 in. diameter
Steering Box	Marles worm and double roller
Propeller Shaft	Open, Hardy Spicer
Rear Axle	Hypoid bevel, Salisbury
Rear Axle – Ratio	3.77 to 1
Rear Axle – Oil Capacity	2 pints
Shock Absorbers	Armstrong piston-type hydraulic

Aston Martin DB Mk III

Aston Martin DB2/4 Mark II Engine

Configuration	Six cylinders in line, overhead valves, twin overhead camshafts
Capacity	2,922 cc
Bore	83 mm
Stroke	90 mm
Compression Ratio	8.16:1
Firing Order	1 – 5 – 3 – 6 – 2 – 4
Valve Timing	io 18° atdc
BHP	140 @ 5,000 rpm
Crankshaft – number of bearings	4
Crankshaft – main bearing	63.5 mm diameter
Crankshaft – big end	51 mm diameter
Ignition Timing	5° btdc
Carburettors	Twin SU 1 ¾ in. HV6
Gearbox - Gear Ratios	3.77, 5.01, 7.45 and 11.0 to 1; reverse 11.0 to 1

Aston Martin DB Mark III Engine

Configuration	Six cylinders in line, overhead valves, twin overhead camshafts
Capacity	2,922 cc
Bore	83 mm
Stroke	90 mm
Compression Ratio	8.16:1
Firing Order	1 – 5 – 3 – 6 – 2 – 4
Valve Timing	io 18° atdc
BHP	162 @ 5,500 rpm
Crankshaft – number of bearings	4
Crankshaft – main bearing	63.5 mm
Crankshaft – big end	51 mm
Ignition Timing	5° btdc
Carburettors	Twin SU 1 ¾ in. H6
Gearbox - Gear Ratios	3.77 (overdrive 2.93), 5.01, 7.45 and 11.0 to 1; reverse 11.0 to 1

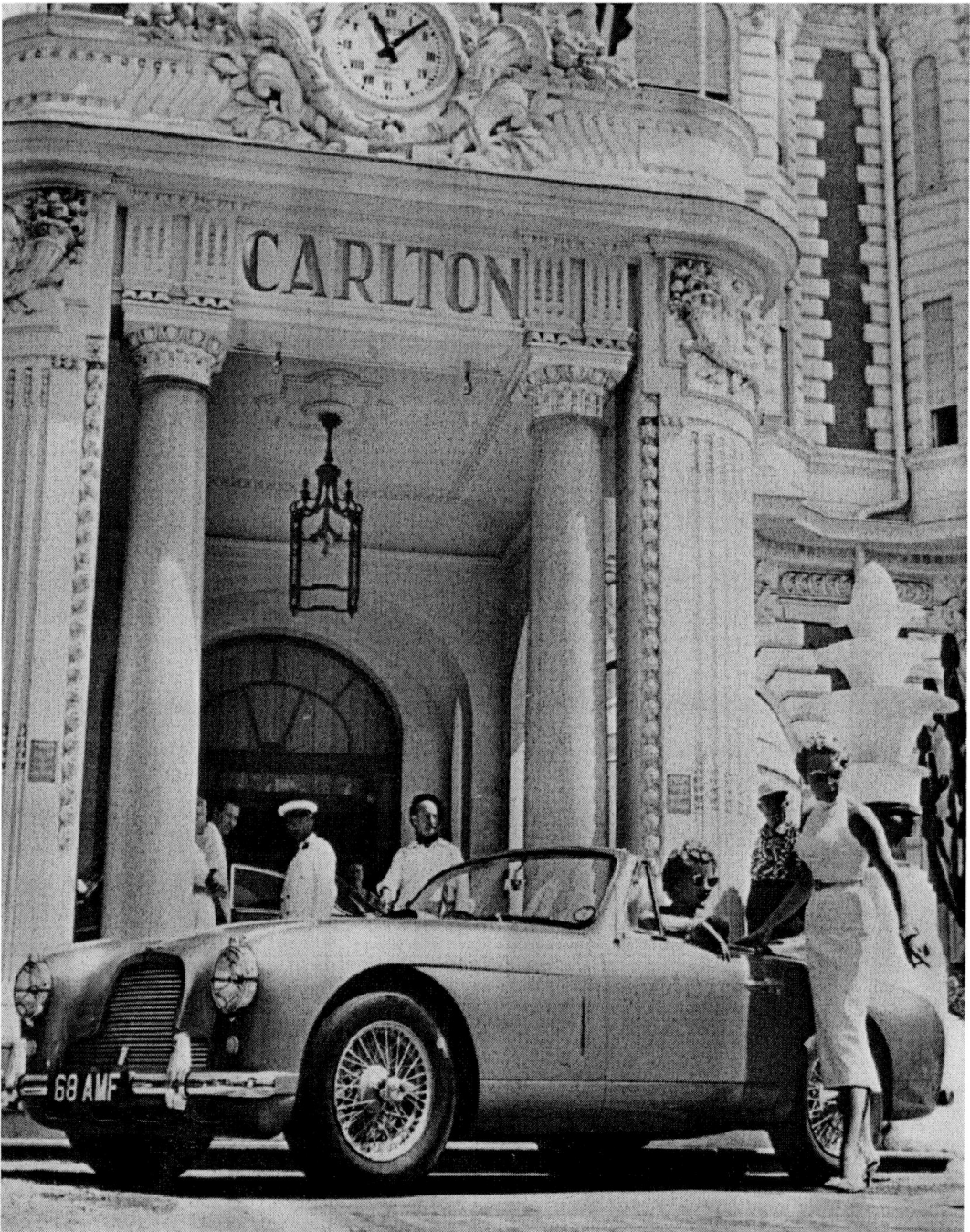

The Aston Martin DB2-4 Drophead Coupe of 1954 pictured outside the Hotel Carlton at Cannes. This is the right-hand drive works demonstrator LML 588

Aston Martin DB2

Aston Martin DB2/4 Bertone

Aston Martin DB2/4 Mark II Chassis

Wheelbase	2515 mm
Track	1372 mm
Length	4356 mm
Width	1651 mm
Weight (dry)	2632 lb
Suspension	Independent at front, live axle at rear, coil springs all round
Wheels and Tyres	Dunlop centre-lock wires, 6.00 x 16 in.
Brakes	Girling 2LS hydraulic, drums 12 in. diameter
Steering Box	Marles worm and double roller
Propeller Shaft	Open, Hardy Spicer
Rea Axle	Hypoid bevel, Salisbury
Rear Axle – Ratio	3.73:1
Rear Axle – Oil Capacity	2.5 pints
Shock Absorbers	Armstrong piston type hydraulic

Aston Martin DB2/4 Mark II Production

Saloon	145
Drophead Coupé	16
Fixed-head Coupé	34
Others	4

Aston Martin DB2/4 Chassis Numbers

Starts at LML/501 and finishes at LML/1065
Produced from October 1953 to October 1955

Aston Martin DB2/4 Mark II Chassis Numbers

Starts at AM300/1101 and finishes at AM300/1299
Produced from October 1955 to August 1957

Aston Martin DB Mark III Chassis

Wheelbase	2515 mm
Track	1372 mm
Length	4356 mm
Width	1651 mm
Weight (dry)	2800 lb
Suspension	Independent at front, live axle at rear, coil springs all round
Wheels and Tyres	Dunlop centre-lock wires, 6.00 x 16 in.
Brakes	Girling hydraulic, 12 in. disc front, 12 in. Alfin drum rear
Steering Box	Marles worm and double roller
Propeller Shaft	Open, Hardy Spicer
Rea Axle	Hypoid bevel, Salisbury
Rear Axle – Ratio	3.77:1
Rear Axle – Oil Capacity	2.5 pints
Shock Absorbers	Armstrong piston type hydraulic

Aston Martin DB2 Production

Saloon	308
Drophead Coupé	98
Others	5

Aston Martin DB2 Chassis Numbers

Starts at LMA/49/1 and finishes at LML/50/406 Produced from May 1950 to April 1953

Aston Martin DB Mark III Production

Saloon	459
Drophead Coupé	85
Fixed-head Coupé	5
Others	2

Aston Martin DB Mark III Chassis Numbers

Starts at AM300/3A/1300 and finishes at AM300/3/1850 Produced from March 1957 to July 1959

The unique Aston Martin DB2/4 Bertone was made for Stanley Harold "Wacky" Arnold.

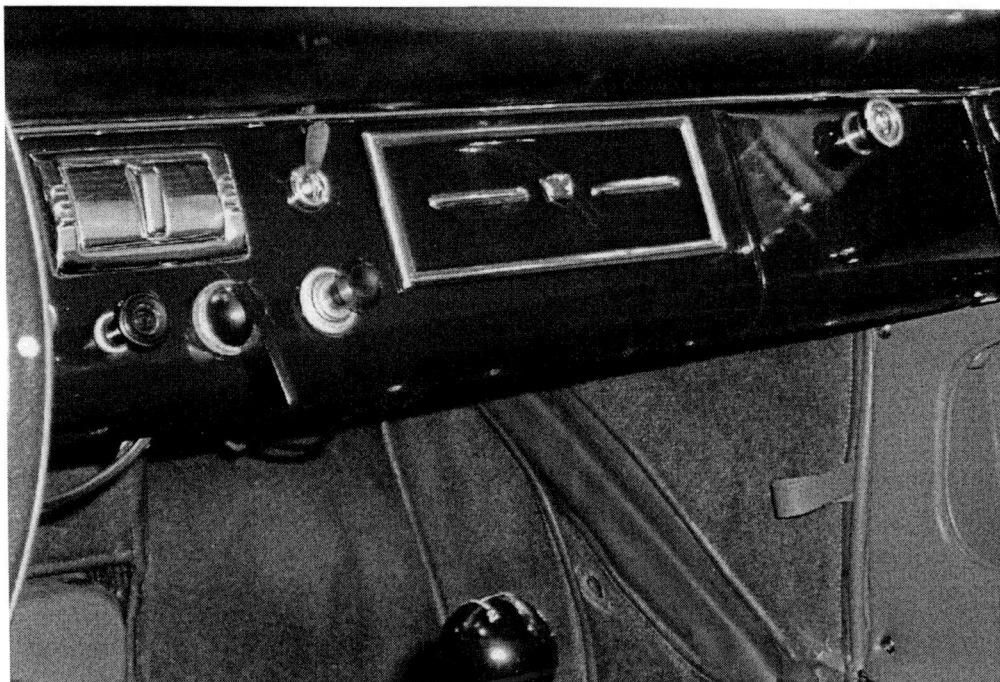

The Bertone-bodied DB2/4 was chassis number LML 762, had engine number VB6J 208 and registration number CSU 844

Aston Martin DB2/4 Allemano Coupe

This DB2/4 Allemano was given chassis number LML/761

Aston Martin DB2/4 Allemano Coupe

The DB2/4 Allemano had engine number VB6J/197

Aston Martin DB2/4 Allemano Coupe

Serafino Allemano had coachworks in Turin and has built many
bodies for different companies since 1935

This DB2/4 Mk II Touring Spyder was chassis number AM300/1162

Aston Martin DB2/4 Touring Spyder

This car was one of only three Touring of Milan Spyders

Aston Martin DB2/4 Touring Spyder

Carrozzeria Touring was established in Milan by former law student Felice Bianchi Anderloni. He was joined by Gaetano Ponzoni; Anderloni was responsible for the styling. Upon Anderloni's death in 1948, Carlo Felice Bianchi Anderloni took his place along with Frederico Formenti. The Aston Martin DB2/4 Spyder of 1956 had its origins in the previous year when Carrozzeria Touring purchased a left-hand drive DB2/4 Mark II chassis and designed a body for it. The drawings were completed by December 1955 and were the work of stylist Frederico Formenti.

Aston Martin DB2 Mulliner

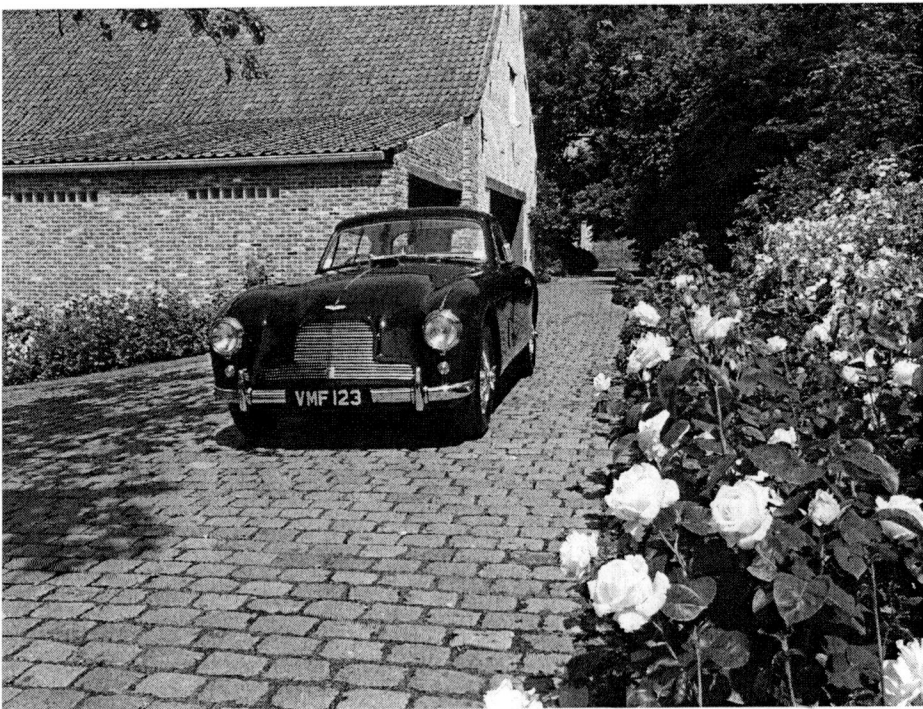

Aston Martin DB2 Mulliner

Aston Martin DB2 Mulliner

Aston Martin DB2 Mulliner

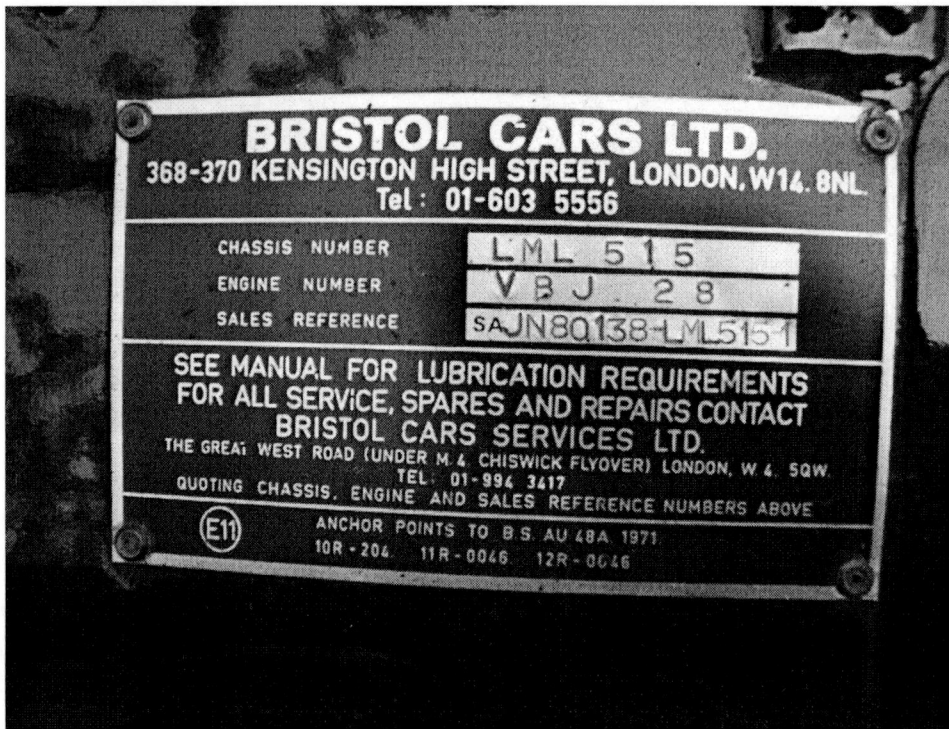

Aston Martin DB2 at the Mille Miglia

Aston Martin DB2 Racing Record

25-26 June 1949	Le Mans 24 Hours	A Jones/ N. Haines	7th overall
9-10 July 1949	Spa 24 Hours (in chassis LMA/49/3)	L. Johnson/ C. Brackenbury	3rd overall
9-10 July 1949	Spa 24 Hours (in chassis LMA/49/1)	L. Macklin/ N. Haines	5th overall
26 March 1950	Inter-Europa Cup, Monza (in chassis LML/49/4)	N. Macklin	2nd
24-25 June 1950	Le Mans 24 Hours (in chassis LML/50/8)	N. Macklin/ G. Abecassis	5th overall
24-25 June 1950	Le Mans 24 Hours (in chassis LML/50/7)	C. Brackenbury/ R. Parnell	6th overall
20 August 1950	Silverstone 1 Hour (in chassis LML/50/8)	R. Sommer	10th overall
20 August 1950	Silverstone 1 Hour (in chassis LML/50/7)	R. Parnell	12th overall
20 August 1950	Silverstone 1 Hour (in chassis LML/50/9)	E. Thompson	15th overall
16 September 1950	Tourist Trophy (in chassis LML/50/7)	R. Parnell	4th overall
16 September 1950	Tourist Trophy (in chassis LML/50/9)	G. Abecassis	5th overall
16 September 1950	Tourist Trophy (in chassis LML/50/8)	L. Macklin	8th overall
28-29 April 1951	Mille Miglia (in chassis LML/50/8)	T.H. Wisdom/ A. Hume	11th overall
5 May 1951	Silverstone 1 Hour (in chassis LML/50/50)	R. Parnell	6th overall
25-26 June 1951	Le Mans 24 Hours (in chassis LML/50/8)	L. Macklin/ E. Thompson	3rd overall
25-26 June 1951	Le Mans 24 Hours (in chassis LML/50/55)	G. Abecassis/ B. Shawe-Taylor	5th overall
25-26 June 1951	Le Mans 24 Hours (in chassis LML/50/50)	R. Parnell/ D. Hampshire	7th overall

Aston Martin DB2

15 September 1951	Tourist Trophy, Dundrod (in chassis LML/50/50)	B. Shawe-Taylor	7th overall
3-4 May 1952	Mille Miglia (in chassis LML/50/8)	T.H. Wisdom/ A. Hume	12th overall
3-4 May 1952	Mille Miglia (in chassis LML/50/55)	G. Abecassis	Retired
18 May 1952	Prix de Berne (in chassis LML/50/55)	G.E. Duke	4th overall
18 May 1952	Prix de Berne (in chassis LML/50/50)	R. Parnell	5th overall
12-13 June 1954	Le Mans 24 Hours (Car number 27 (LML 693) an Aston Martin DB2/4 completed 122 laps in the Sports 3000 Group)	Hermano da Silva Ramos/ Jean-Paul Colas	Did not finish
30 April – 1 May 1955	Mille Miglia (Aston Martin DB2/4 was car number 441)	Hermano da Silva Ramos/ Jean Claude Vidilles	16th place
30 April – 1 May 1955	Mille Miglia (Aston Martin DB2/4 was car number 418)	Paul Frere/ Louis Klemantaski	Did not finish
30 April – 1 May 1955	Mille Miglia (Aston Martin DB2/4 was car number 436)	Tommy Wisdom/ Peter Bolton	Did not finish
26 January 1958	Buenos Aires 1000 kms	Patricio Badaracco/ Federico Mayol	Did not finish
22 March 1958	Sebring 12 Hours (Car number 26, an Aston Martin DB2/4 Mk III completed 15 laps in the Grand Touring Group)	George Constantine/ John Dalton	Did not finish
6 May 1962	Targa Florio (Car number 80 was an Aston Martin DB2/4)	Edward Wray/ Dick Crosfield	Did not finish

Aston Martin DB3

Aston Martin got Von Eberhorst to design a Sports-Racing Car that used the existing LMB 2.6 litre engine and a David Brown 5-speed gearbox. The Aston Martin DB3 had a ladder-type chassis made from 16-gauge four-inch tubes. The front suspension used trailing links and transverse torsion bars, but the rear suspension used a de Dion rear axle. The Aston Martin DB3 had an aluminium-panelled body but had the lines of a touring car. It looked like a completely open version of the Aston Martin DB2 apart from the fact that it had a portcullis radiator grille. When raced initially the Aston Martin DB3 had three Weber 35 DCO carburettors but was only capable of developing 133 bhp at 5500 rpm. In 1952 this changed to 36 DCFS carburettors and then the car was given the S527S gearbox in place of the S527 gearbox.

Dashboard and instruments of the Aston Martin DB3

Aston Martin DB3 Racing Record

15 September 1951	Tourist Trophy (DB3/1)	L. Macklin	Retired
10 May 1952	Silverstone (DB3/3)	R. Parnell	2nd
10 May 1952	Silverstone (DB3/5)	G. Abercassis	3rd
10 May 1952	Silverstone (DB3/5)	L. Macklin	4th
10 May 1952	Silverstone (DB3/1)	G.E. Duke	Retired
29 May 1952	British Empire Trophy (DB3/1)	G.E. Duke	Retired
2 June 1952	Monaco Grand Prix (DB3/4)	P.J. Collins	7th
2 June 1952	Monaco Grand Prix (DB3/3)	R. Parnell	Retired
2 June 1952	Monaco Grand Prix (DB3/5)	L. Macklin	Retired
14-15 June 1952	Le Mans 24 Hours (DB3/1)	R. Parnell/ Eric Thompson	Retired
14-15 June 1952	Le Mans 24 Hours (DB3/3)	R.D. Poore/ P.D.C. Griffith	Retired
14-15 June 1952	Le Mans 24 Hours (DB3/5)	L. Macklin/ P.J. Collins	Retired
10 July 1952	Jersey Road Race (DB3/4)	G. Abecassis	3rd
10 July 1952	Jersey Road Race (DB3/5)	R. Parnell	4th
2 August 1952	Int. Sports Car Race (DB3/4)	R. Parnell	3rd
2 August 1952	Int. Sports Car Race (DB3/4)	G. Abecassis	Retired
16 August 1952	Goodwood 9 Hours Race (DB3/5)	P.J. Collins/ P.D.C. Griffith	1st

Aston Martin DB3

16 August 1952	Goodwood 9 Hours Race (DB3/4)	G. Abecassis/ P.D. Moore	Retired
16 August 1952	Goodwood 9 Hours Race	R. Parnell/ Eric Thompson	Retired
8 March 1953	Sebring 12 Hours (DB3/5)	R. Parnell/ G. Abecassis	2nd
8 March 1953	Sebring 12 Hours (DB3/4)	P.J. Collins/ G.E. Duke	Retired
25-26 April 1953	Mille Miglia (DB3/3)	R. Parnell/ L. Klementaski	5th
25-26 April 1953	Mille Miglia (DB3/4)	P.J. Collins/ M. Keen	16th
25-26 April 1953	Mille Miglia (DB3/5)	G. Abecassis/ P.D.C. Griffith	Retired
9 May 1953	Silverstone (DB3/3)	R. Parnell	3rd
9 May 1953	Silverstone (DB3/4)	P.J. Collins	4th
9 May 1953	Silverstone (DB3/2)	G.E. Duke	Retired
20 December 1953	Casablanca 12 Hours (DB3/3)	R.F. Salvadori/ M. Sparken	4th

Aston Martin DB3 Gallery

This car is chassis DB3/5 and is registered UPL 4

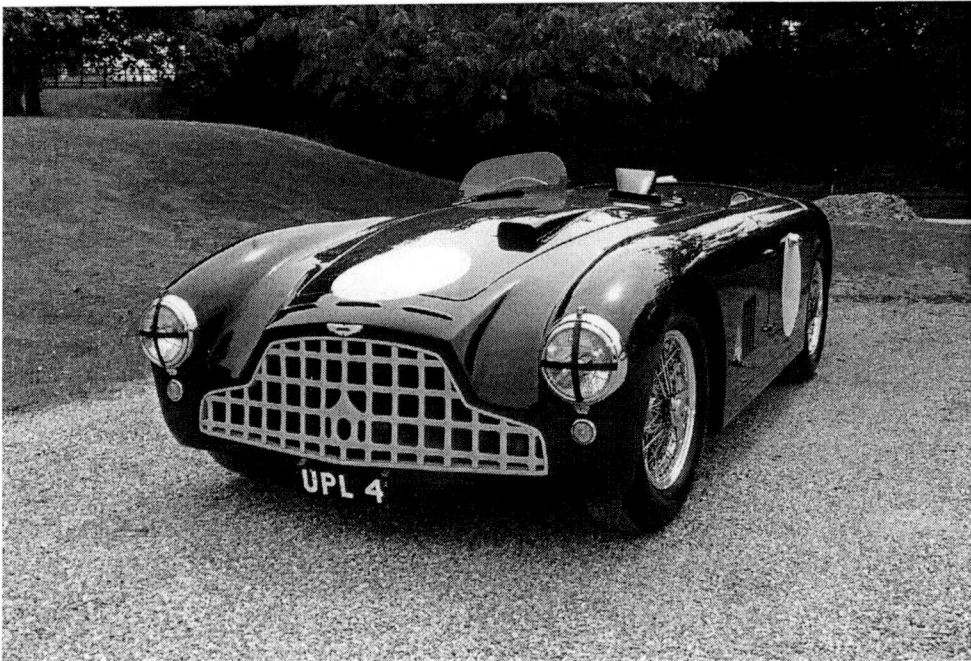

Chassis DB3/5 came 1st at the Goodwood 9 Hr Race in August 1952

Chassis DB3/5 also came 2nd at Sebring 12 Hr Race in March 1953

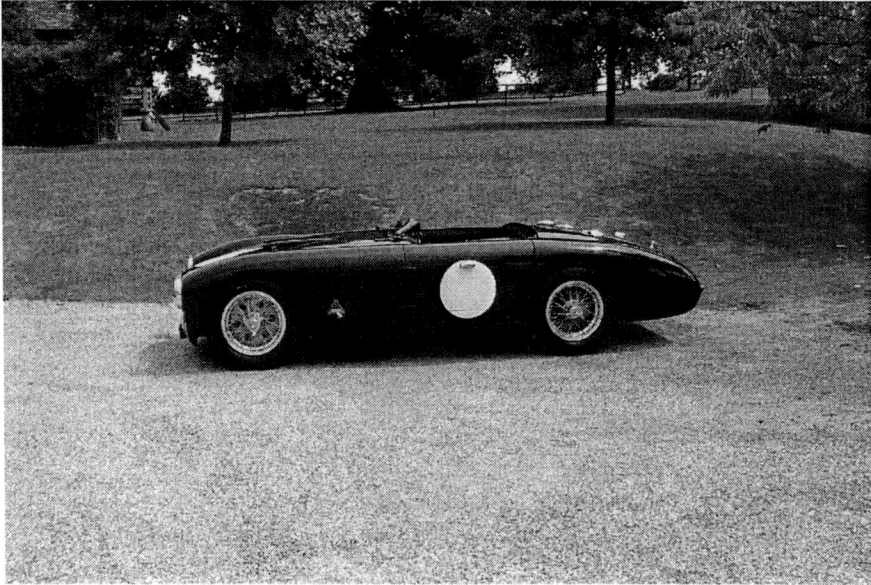

At Boreham in August 1952, Parnell drove DB3/5. He won the 3000cc class of the sports car race and finished third overall in the above car.

The cockpit of the Aston Martin DB3/5

Aston Martin DB3

Superb engine bay of the Aston Martin DB3/5

Webers of the Aston Martin DB3

Engine bay of the Aston Martin DB3

Foot pedals of the Aston Martin DB3

Aston Martin DB3 Specifications

Engine:	6-Cylinder Twin Overhead Camshaft 2580 cc (78 mm x 90 mm) with three Weber twin-choke 36 DCF5 carburettors
Compression Ratio:	8.16 to 1
Power Output:	140 bhp at 5200 rpm

Gearbox Ratios:

Top:	3.415 to 1
Fourth:	4.11 to 1
Third:	5.24 to 1
Second:	7.768 to 1
First:	11.919 to 1
Reverse:	8.63 to 1

Final Drive:	David Brown hypoid bevel, ratio 4.11 to 1

Chassis: Twin-tubular and constructed from 4 inch 16-gauge chrome molybdenum longitudinal members. Three 5 inch 14-gauge cross-members

Front Suspension: Independent by trailing links and transverse torsion bars

Rear Suspension: De Dion axle, trailing links and torsion bars

Wheels: 16 inch centre-lock wire type

Overall Length: 13 feet 2 ½ inches
Overall Width: 5 feet 1 ½ inches
Overall Height: 3 feet 4 inches to include height of aero screen

Aston Martin DB4 Tickford

Aston Martin DB4

With a top speed of over 140 mph and a price in Britain of over £4,000, the Aston Martin DB4 truly can be said to live up to its makers' claim "…the ultimate symbol of success." Though cars capable of even higher speed have passed through the hands of *The Autocar* – only two, in fact – the DB4 is the fastest production four-seater yet tested.

Since this model was first introduced in October 1958, using a direct development of the six-cylinder 3.7-litre engine that made its debut in the DBR2-370 sports-racing car at Le Mans the previous year, two series modifications have been announced. The first was in April this year, when Laycock-de Normanville overdrive was made available; three final drive ratios were then listed, 3.54, 3.77 and 4.09 to 1, overdrive being available only with the latter two.

The latest series, which were embodied in the car under test, include a new type of two-plate Borg and Beck clutch, and the option of a 3.31 to 1 final drive ratio, without overdrive, of course; the 4.09 to 1 ratio has been dropped. In addition, the ratios of second and third gear have been lowered numerically by 12 per cent, and a modified radiator grille replaces the original pattern with narrow, closely spaced horizontal slats.

On first getting into the car – not too easy, as the very wide doors open only to about 45 degrees – one is immediately impressed by the attention to detail, and the functional layout and finish. Everything save the chrome instrument bexels is black and non-reflecting, the leather of the upholstery, scuttle, fascia and the padded roll along its top edge, and the matt finish for the instrument surround; even the spokes of the lightweight, alloy-and-laminated-wood steering wheel are in matt black.

The very full quota of dials id grouped directly ahead of the driver in a hooded panel, clearly visible when the road wheels are in the straight-ahead position. Markings on the rev-counter and speedometer are large, and easily taken in at a glance, the whole layout reflecting years of competition work behind this car. The driving compartment is divided fore-and-aft by the high hump covering the clutch and gearbox, and the short, rigid gear-lever is placed precisely where the left hand drops to it.

The view through the wide, sloping screen is excellent and the screen pillars are thin; there is very little distortion at the side extremities of the screen, despite a fairly extensive wrap-around. A comprehensive heating-ventilating system is fitted, with a central control in the middle of the fascia and overriding quadrant levers at either side of the front compartment, alongside the driver's and passenger's knees, to govern the quantity and direction of air; all these controls operate smoothly and precisely. Complete and very powerful ventilation of the car with fresh air, throughout the range from hot to cold, can be achieved by means of this system; air is admitted through ducts to the interior, and out through the hinged quarter-ventilators, so that there is no need to open the winding windows. The system fitted to this car is one of the most efficient and comprehensive that we have yet tried.

Reutter seats, with a wide range of fore-and-aft adjustment, are standard; in addition, the rake of the backrests is adjustable right to the near horizontal position. Driver comfort and posture being of great importance in such a car, the steering wheel has two positions of fore-and-aft adjustment, and the angle of the column can also be altered, so that it is possible to tailor the position to suit all shapes and sizes. The driver sits high, though with adequate head-clearance, very much in command of the car.

Among the detail fittings are a two-speed wiper control and a rheostat for the instrument lighting. The wipers, with twin rubber in each blade, continued to sweep regularly and remained in contact with the screen even at the car's maximum speed, though a quicker sweep in the "fast" position would be desirable. Further attention to detail is shown in the coat-hanger hooks (unusual in British cars) provided at each side of the car, at roof level.

The body cannot be strictly regarded as more than an occasional four-seater, and it would not be in the interests of a happy crew to embark on long journeys with more than three people in the car, as head and leg room at the back are very limited. However, the rear compartment is fully and comfortably upholstered, and four people can be carried, if at the pardonable expense of the front passenger's leg-room, and the less acceptable sacrifice of the driver's ideal position. Access to the rear compartment is gained without much contortion by tilting the backrests of the front seats fully forward.

The engine starts from cold immediately, and no choke was required in mild weather; it can be brought up to its working temperature very quickly by means of the radiator blind, controlled from the cockpit. Most impressive features are its smoothness and extreme tractability in traffic. Despite giving a top speed of over 140 m.p.h., it can trickle along without a snatch at 15 m.p.h. in top gear (or 10 m.p.h. in third), pulling away smoothly as the throttle is opened, all of which makes it a pleasant, docile car for town use.

Engine and exhaust noises in the car are reasonably subdued, and it is possible to maintain conversation without shouting except when travelling at over 110 m.p.h. Above this speed, one becomes aware that a good deal is going on beneath the bonnet, and at around 4,700 r.p.m. the increased noise is accompanied by slight vibration. Wind noise at high speeds is more than one would expect with such an aerodynamic body. The exhaust noise is not obtrusive, though it is just sufficiently loud to be audible to the driver and to help materially in gear changing. Rear seat passengers, however, are subjected to some booming from the exhaust, and on this car, towards to end of the test, an unpleasant "fluffing" developed on the overrun from the twin exhausts at low revs.

Torque at low engine speeds is not great, and it is not until 4,000 r.p.m. are reached that the power really comes in which it does with a most electrifying effect.

The result is that if the excellent performance is to be enjoyed, full use must be made of the gearbox, the ratios of which are very well spaced indeed; second and third speeds will take the car up to 76 and 115 m.p.h. respectively, at the recommended limit of 5,800 r.p.m. (6,000 in top). It is only when one grows accustomed to driving the car that one learns to make full use of second gear. In normal main road traffic, moving at approximately 60 m.p.h., every possible opportunity for overtaking can be used, the car positively leaping forward in this gear. With the lower axle ratios available, this intermediate gear acceleration would be even more impressive, though at the cost of a small reduction in maximum speed.

The maximum speed seen during the test runs, of 141 m.p.h. in one direction, was achieved at an engine speed of 5,750 r.p.m. the road speed being indicated on an independent electric speedometer accurate at this speed to within 0.1 m.p.h. This suggests that the rear axle ratio of 3.31 to 1 is just about right where all-out maximum speed is the owner's prime requirement. In view of the repeated high-speed runs at 140 m.p.h. or more required during the test, the manufacturers fitted Dunlop R5

racing tyres, of the dry weather type, instead of the Avon Turbospeeds fitted as standard.

Cruising speed is governed only by road conditions, the car appearing perfectly happy and relaxed at 120 m.p.h., or 4,850 r.p.m. – a figure which does not quite tie up with the makers' figure of 24.2 m.p.h. per 1,000 r.p.m. in top gear, due to the slightly larger rolling radius of the Dunlop R5 tyres.

To some extent, the acceleration figures may not reflect fully the exciting performance for, on the car tested, the gear change was "notchy," stiff and offered overmuch resistance, perhaps because the car had done only a low mileage. The synchromesh on all four speeds was strong, and impossible to override, and had full-throttle changes been possible, there is little doubt that the figures would have shown an improvement. Moreover, the gear change was not consistent; sometimes, in normal use, the lever would slip through cleanly and easily, and at others one had to take a second bite. Towards the end of the test period, however, it began to ease up appreciably.

The clutch pedal travel is too long for comfort; and, due to the increased drag of multi-plate clutches, the pedal always has to be depressed fully before first gear can be engaged with the car at rest; the pedal pressure, too, is high and becomes tiring in traffic when full depression is required frequently. In performance, however, it was pleasantly smooth and progressive, well up to the power of the engine, and at no time did it show any signs of slipping.

Steering is quick, positive and without any lost motion or friction, though the slight and desirable understeer made it rather heavy on tight, fast bends unless the back was helped round by use of the throttle. Directional stability was arrow-like and superb, the car maintaining a dead-straight line, hands-off, at speeds approaching its maximum, even in the wet. This quality, however, was very much influenced by tyre pressures, a few pounds reduction in the rear tyres affecting it appreciably.

Though the steering does transmit road shocks to a minor extent, it does not react uncomfortably; directional stability is much affected by longitudinal irregularities, such as tram-lines or the edges of newly surfaced sections of road, but the steep camber of continental roads does not influence it. Handling is not altered noticeably by the extensive variations in weight behind the rear axle of a full, or empty, fuel tank, with its capacity of 19 gallons.

By sports car standards of a few years ago, the suspension is soft, and it absorbs the long-frequency undulations on main roads, providing a steady and comfortable ride. Over more acute, high-frequency irregularities, particularly with an empty fuel tank, the ride was less comfortable, though the body insulation cuts out much of the road noise.

Despite the relative softness of the suspension, any incitement to pitch is damped out effectively, even to the extent of the nose-down or tail-down attitudes normally adopted under heavy braking or acceleration. There is very little roll, however fast the car is cornered; such as there is serves as a warning that one is approaching the limit of adhesion. There are no vices or idiosyncrasies in the handling, and one quickly acquires a sense of confidence that, whatever liberties one takes within reason, the car will help one out of trouble. When in the wet the rear wheels were induced to slide outwards, correction was extremely quick and easy. On rough surfaces it was sometimes difficult to anticipate tail movements.

On a car of this sort, brakes play an all-important part, and the Aston Martin's hydraulic, servo-assisted Dunlop discs produced some of the best retardation figures recorded in *The Autocar* road tests. Because of the "hard" pads, however, there is the reservation that they have little "bite" when first applied when the discs are cool. The efficiency quickly builds up with temperature and the brakes become immensely sure and powerful, pulling the car up quickly in a dead straight line. They inspire complete confidence and did not appear to deteriorate during the testing.

The hand-brake, of the pull-up "fly off" pattern, is well placed horizontally to the right of the driving seat. Working on the rear discs only, it could not quite hold the car forwards or backwards on the 1-in-4 test gradient.

At night, on relatively traffic-free roads, the car is in its element, and it is perhaps in such conditions that one obtains the greatest pleasure from driving it. The Lucas Le Mans headlamps give sufficient range and spread for high cruising speeds. With the rheostat, the panel lighting can be reduced to the barest minimum, and the pleasant black finish of everything surrounding the driver is extremely restful. There are no disconcerting reflections on the screen at night, though in daylight the steering wheel rim does reflect. In such conditions, one can put up surprising averages, not by cornering excessively fast, or taking chances through built-up areas, but by using the wonderful indirect-gear performance whenever the headlamps reach forward to a stretch of clear straight road. In the dipped position, there is only a reasonable range.

Aston Martin DB4 Bertone "Jet"

The Aston Martin DB4 GT chassis 0201L with Bertone coachwork as it appeared at the Turin Show of 1961. It had previously appeared at the 1961 Geneva Show.

Aston Martin DB4 Bertone "Jet"

The Aston Martin DB4 Bertone "Jet" was the last DB4 GT chassis built and was chassis number 0201. It was built by Bertone for the 1961 Geneva Show and is currently owned by Swiss Aston Martin enthusiast Hans-Peter Weidemann. The car spent much time prior to this in Beirut and was owned by Sarkis Najjarian.

To the right of the steering column, within finger reach of the wheel, is a stalk which operates the indicators in the left-right plane, and flashes (or dips) the headlamps when moved upwards towards the wheel. A two-tone horn, for town and country use, would be a welcome refinement, for the existing "audible warning" is scarcely penetrating enough for clearing the way on high-speed motor-roads. Some may consider that a small central horn button is not over-convenient.

The luggage locker, softly carpeted and free from obstructions, has ample capacity for the needs of two; the battery is carried to the right, behind a panel with quick-action fasteners; the tools fit neatly into a recess on the opposite side, and are of the highest quality, and comprehensive. A reversing lamp operated automatically when reverse gear is selected, is mounted on the locker lid, combined with the registration plate lamp. The fuel filler cap – in fact, a small panel combining the cap – is set in the body at waist level, behind the left-side ventilator window. It is released by means of a finger-pull in the roof, near the left door post so that, when the car is locked, the tank is locked automatically as well. Out of keeping with the general excellent quality of the accessories and fittings are the interior lamps with integral switches one at each side of the roof. The door-operated courtesy switches, however, are very well made and are adjustable.

Under-bonnet accessibility is excellent, the radiator header tank and filler cap being mounted to the left of the opening, and the oil-level dipstick being extended right up to the level of the valve covers. The oil-filler cap is to the front of the valve covers, recessed in the aluminium cowling to the fan. A remarkably comprehensive instruction book, leather bound and gold tooled, in keeping with the rest of the car, tells the owner all he could possibly require.

The DB4 is an ideal long-distance touring car, in which great distances can be covered in amazingly short times; a Grand Tourer, in fact, though the manufacturers reserve this title for the even hotter DB4-GT two seater. It is reasonably quite, and its performance and controllability are of a very high order, so that it is a constant pleasure to drive. The controls, at least on the car tested, were a little on the heavy side, but at over 27 cwt. it is not a light car. By any standards it is tractable and flexible – to a remarkable extent for a car with this performance. And being, as it were, permanently in the public eye like all exceptional cars, it encourages one to drive it courteously and well in towns and in crowded traffic conditions, for one knows that, as soon as the open road is reached, one can accelerate clear and pass the lot!

Aston Martin DB4 Data

Price (basic), with two-door saloon body **£2,800**
British purchase tax **£1,284 11s 5d**
Total (in Great Britain) **£4,084 11s 5d**

Extras (including p.t.); Radio **£43 10s 0d**
Overdrive **£60**

Engine Capacity — 3,670 c.c. (223.8 cu. in.)
Number of cylinders — 6
Bore and Stroke — 92x92 mm (3.62x3.62 in.)
Valve gear — Twin overhead camshafts
Compression ration — 8.25 to 1
B.H.P. — 240 (net) at 5,500 r.p.m.
B.H.P. per ton laden — 158.3
Torque — 240 lb. ft. at 4,250 r.p.m.
M.P.H. per 1,000 r.p.m. in top gear — 24.2

Weight (with 5 gallons of fuel) — 27.4 cwt (3,070 lb.)
Weight distribution (per cent) — Front 51.2, Rear 48.8
Laden as tested — 30.4 cwt (3,406 lb.)
Lb. per c.c. (laden) — 0.93

Brakes Type   Dunlop discs
    Method of operation   Hydraulic, vacuum servo-
                                           assisted
    Disc diameter   Front 12.12 in.
                                           Rear 11.12 in.
    Swept area   Front 287.2 sq. in.
                                           Rear 236.8 236.8 sq. in.
                                           345 sq. in. per ton laden

Tyres   6.00-16 in. R5 Dunlop
    Pressures (p.s.i.)   Front 26, Rear 28 (normal)
                                           Front 33, Rear 35 (fast)

Tank Capacity   19 imperial gallons
                                           Reserve 3 gallons
    Oil sump   21 pints
    Cooling system   28 pints (including heater)

Dimensions Wheelbase   8ft. 2in.
    Track   Front 4ft. 6in.
                                           Rear 4ft. 5.5 in.
    Length (overall)   14ft. 8.75in.
    Width   5ft. 6in.
    Height   4ft. 4in.
    Ground clearance   6.25 in.

Electrical System   12-volt, 51 ampere-hour
                                           battery
    Head lamps   45-40 watt bulbs

Suspension Front   Transverse wishbones, co-
                                           axial coil springs and
                                           telescopic dampers
    Rear   Live axle, coil springs,
                                           parallel trailing links and
                                           transverse Watts linkage,
                                           lever-type dampers

Aston Martin DB4 Performance

Acceleration Times (mean)
Speed Range, Gear Ratios and Time in Seconds

MPH	3.31 To 1	4.14 to 1	6.14 to 1	9.67 to 1
10-30		6.9	4.4	2.8
20-40	8.2	6.4	4.2	2.6
30-50	8.2	6.2	3.9	
40-60	8.9	6.4	3.9	
50-70	8.7	6.5	3.8	
60-80	9.0	6.6		
70-90	9.1	6.6		
80-100	10.5	7.2		
90-110	11.1	7.9		
100-120	13.7			
110-130	17.4			

From rest through gears to:

30 m.p.h.	3.5 seconds
40 m.p.h.	4.9 seconds
50 m.p.h.	6.7 seconds
60 m.p.h.	8.5 seconds
70 m.p.h.	10.6 seconds
80 m.p.h.	12.5 seconds
90 m.p.h.	17.7 seconds
100 m.p.h.	21.7 seconds
110 m.p.h.	26.0 seconds
120 m.p.h.	34.6 seconds
130 m.p.h.	44.8 seconds

Standing quarter mile   16.1 seconds

Maximum Speeds on Gears

Gear		m.p.h.	k.p.h.
Top	(mean)	140.6	226.3
	(best)	141.0	226.9
3rd		115.0	185.0
2nd		76.0	122.0
1st		46.0	74.0

Tractive Effort (by Tapley meter)

	Pull (lb. per ton)	Equivalent gradient
Top	320	1 in 6.9
Third	413	1 in 5.3
Second	640	1 in 3.4

Brakes (at 30 m.p.h. in neutral)

Pedal load In lb.	Retardation	Equiv. stopping distance in ft.
25	0.17g	168
50	0.39g	77
75	0.70g	43
100	1.00g	30

Fuel Consumption (at steady speeds in top gear)

30 m.p.h.	30.7 m.p.g.
40 m.p.h.	28.3 m.p.g.
50 m.p.h.	24.9 m.p.g.
60 m.p.h.	22.3 m.p.g.
70 m.p.h.	19.5 m.p.g.
80 m.p.h.	18.2 m.p.g.
90 m.p.h.	17.3 m.p.g.
100 m.p.h.	15.9 m.p.g.
110 m.p.h.	14.0 m.p.g.

Aston Martin DB4 Gallery

Aston Martin DB4

Aston Martin DB4 GT

The Aston Martin DB4 GT was introduced at the 1959 British Motor Show and was distinguishable by the fact that it had a deeper bonnet scoop, lightweight Borrani wheels and was 5 inches shorter in the wheelbase compared to the standard Aston Martin DB4.

The DB4 GT had plexiglass rear windows and slightly simpler trim and its crankcase and block were made of RR50 alloy.

The Aston Martin DB4 GT was 180lb lighter than the DB4, it had an increased compression ratio of 9 to 1, higher-lift camshafts, three twin-choke side-draught Webers and twin plugs per cylinder fed by dual distributors.

The Aston Martin DB4 GT had 302 bhp at 6000 rpm and 240lb ft of torque at 5000 rpm.

Aston Martin DB4 GT's had chassis numbers that Stable used two lightweight GTs, 0125 and 0151. These cars had the registration number 18 TVX and 17 TVX. Both were entered in the 1960 Tourist Trophy, driven by Roy

Acceleration in Each Gear				
	Jaguar E-Type		Aston Martin DB4GT	
mph	Top	3rd	Top	3rd
10-30				
20-40		3.9		6.1
30-50	5.2	4.3	7.7	6.3
40-60	5.8	4.3	8.3	6.3
50-70	6.1	3.9	8.7	5.7
60-80	5.5	4.9	7.9	5.7
70-90	5.7		8.5	5.8
80-100	7.3		9.2	6.4
90-110			9.6	

started at DB4 GT/0101/L up to DB4 GT/0201/L. However, numbers 0192, 0194 and 1098 were not used. Seventy-five Aston Martin DB4 GT's were produced of which six were special lightweight cars. John Ogier and his Essex Racing Salvadori and Innes Ireland.

Aston Martin DB4 GT 0124/R, registration number 587 GJB with engine number 3700154GT was the lightweight driven by Stirling Moss at Goodwood in 1960 and which set a new lap record.

Above chassis number 0125/R which was registered 18 TVX

Comparisons			
	Aston DB4 GT	**Porsche 928**	**4.2 E-Type**
Power	302 bhp	330 bhp	265 bhp
Torquw	240 lb ft	317 lb ft	283 lb ft
Weight	2800 lb	3449 lb	2892 lb
Top Speed	152.5 mph	165 mph	153 mph
0-60	6.4 secs	5.6 secs	7.6 secs
Price	£45,521	£62,626	£17,243

Aston Martin DB4 Zagato

Of the 19 Aston Martin Zagato DB4 GTs built in the 1960 to 1963 period, four chassis numbers (0192, 0196, 0197 and 0198) were allocated but not built at that time.

They were subsequently built under the supervision of former Aston Martin factory man Richard Williams. Former Aston Martin Team manager Richard Williams believes you could not tell the older and the later built Aston Martin Zagatos.

Victor Gauntlett acknowledged that "the integrity is convincing". Only the four spare chassis numbers allocated at the time were taken up. And it was in 1987 that Victor Gauntlett and Peter Livanos decided that the cars for the four spare chassis numbers would be built. They were built in the old way with the rolling chassis being sent to Zagato in Italy for the bodies to be fabricated and fitted.

By 1989, Richard Williams had completed the rolling chassis. His own original Aston Martin DB4 GT Zagato was sent out to Italy and used as a model. Of the four cars, three had Zagato style bonnets (featuring the three-hump Zagato style) while one had a Richard Williams styled bonnet looking more Aston Martin. The Sanction II Zagatos, as the cars have come to be known, were built at Richard Williams' premises in Cobham, Surrey and have 4.2 litre engines rather than the 3.7 litre engines of the original Aston Martin DB4 Zagatos. Additionally, experience has proved that the 45DCOE4 carburettors perform better with extended inlet manifolds and therefore these have been fitted to the four DB4 GT Sanction II Zagato cars. The geometry of the front suspension was also slightly altered on the later four cars and they weighed 2515lbs as against 2550lbs of the 1960's cars.

The transmission is standard on the "new" Aston Martin DB4 GT Zagatos (0192, 0196, 0197, 0198) with Borg and Beck twin-plate clutch, David Brown close ratio four speed gearbox and 3.54 to 1 Salisbury live rear axle with a Power-Lok limited slip differential. The Sanction II cars featured the use of alternators instead of dynamos.

The back axle is braced by tubes, welded on the nose of the differential and stretching back out towards the hubs. The hubs have double wheel bearings. Road holding on the Sanction II cars should be somewhat superior to that of the original 1960s DB4 Zagatos.

Rear light arrangement varied somewhat from car to car

Wood-trimmed steering wheel in the Aston Martin Zagato is similar to that used in Touring-bodied GTs

Engine compartment air outlet is made more attractive with the Zagato badge

The engine of the Aston Martin DB4 GT Zagato

Aston Martin DB4 Zagato

The front end of the Aston Martin DB4 Zagato shows an additional air
intake for the oil cooler below the radiator

Aston Martin DB4 Zagato Race Record

Date	Race	Drivers	Position
10-11 Jun 61	Le Mans 24 Hours (Car no. 1 in race, Chassis 0180/L)	Jean Kerguen/ Jacques Dewez/ Jean-Paul Colas	Not running at finish
10-11 Jun 61	Le Mans 24 Hours (Car no. 3 in race, Chassis 0183/R)	Lex Davison/ Bob Stilwell	Did not finish (engine)
10-11 Jun 61	Le Mans 24 Hours (Car no. 2 in race, Chassis 0182/R)	Jack Fairman/ Bernard Consten	Did not finish (engine)
19 Aug 61	Tourist Trophy (GB) (Car no. 1 in race, Reg. 1 VEV, Chassis 0182/R, completed 108 laps)	Roy Salvadori	3rd
19 Aug 61	Tourist Trophy (GB) (Car no. 3 in race, Reg. 2 VEV, Chassis 0183/R, completed 107 laps)	Jim Clark	4th
10 Sep 61	Monza Coppa Inter-Europa (Car no. 68 in race, Reg. 1 VEV, Chassis 0182/R, completed 93 laps)	Tony Maggs	2nd
10 Sep 61	Monza Coppa Inter-Europa (Car no. 62 in race, Chassis 0180/R, completed 89 laps)	Jean Kerguen	4th
22 Oct 61	Paris 1000kms (Car no. 15 in race, Chassis 0182/R, completed 126 laps)	Jim Clark/ Innes Ireland	6th
22 Oct 61	Paris 1000kms (Car no. 14 in race, completed 120 laps)	Jean Kerguen/ Jacques Dewez	14th

Date	Race	Drivers	Position
23-24 Jun 62	Le Mans 24 Hours (Car no. 12 in race, Chassis 0193, completed 134 laps)	Jean Kerguen/ Jacques Dewez	Did not finish (engine)
23-24 Jun 62	Le Mans 24 Hours (Car no. 14 in race, Chassis 0200, completed 124 laps)	Mike Salmon/ Ian B. Baillie	Did not finish (engine)
15-16 Jun 63	Le Mans 24 Hours (Car no. 19 in race, Chassis 0193)	Jacques Dewez/ Jean Kerguen	Did not finish (axle)
7 Jul 63	Auvergne Trophy (Car no. 1, Chassis 0193, completed 41 laps)	Jean Kerguen	18th
11 Oct 64	Paris 1000kms (Car no. 12 in race, Chassis 0183/R)	Andrew Hedges/ John Turner	Did not finish (gearbox)

One Aston Martin DB4 Zagato (Chassis 0201L) was given a Bertone coupe body in 1961

Other Aston Martin Zagatos were bought and used by private owners in 1962. E. Portman ran the Aston Martin DB4 Zagato (Chassis 0117R) in the BARC. Additionally, John Coombs bought new the Aston Martin DB4 Zagato (Chassis 0190L) and drove it with Salvadori at a BRSCC meeting at Brands Hatch in May.

Aston Martin DB4 GT

This Aston Martin DB4 GT is chassis number DB4GT/0126/GT

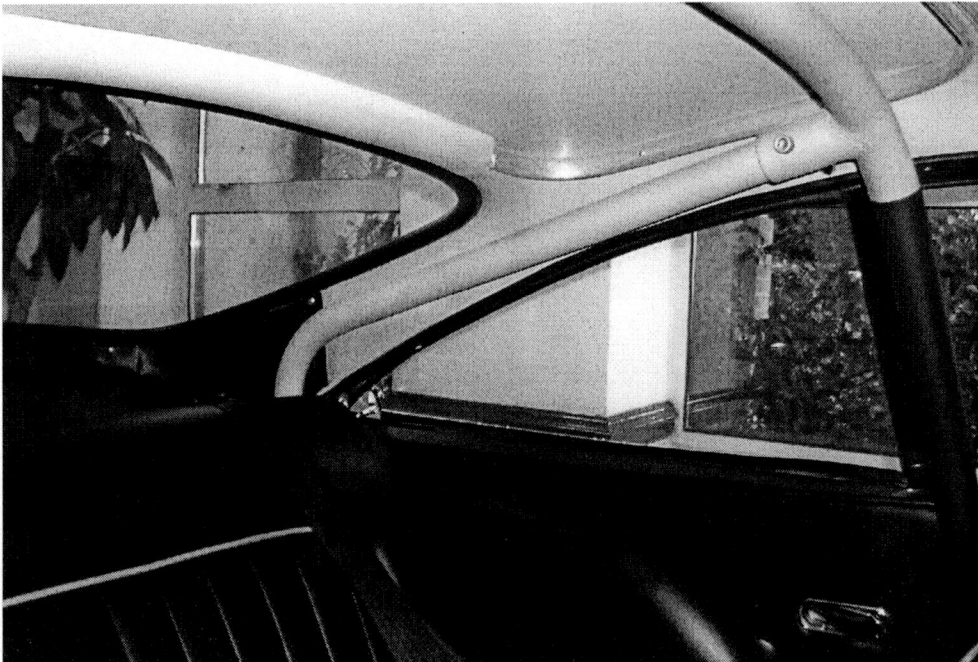

This DB4 GT is one of only three GTs fitted with rear seats

Aston Martin DB4 GT

This Aston Martin DB4 GT has engine number 370/0126/GT

The Aston Martin DB4 GT has Borrani wheels

Aston Martin DB4 GT

This well-known Aston Martin DB4 GT race car has chassis number DP199/1

This car has engine number 370/0184/GT

Aston Martin DB4 In Competition

Date	Event	Driver	Chassis	Result
3 March 1973	Midland AC Meeting	I.H. Masson	DB4/239/R (Reg WLE 358)	7th Overall
24 March 1973	Jaguar D.C. Meeting	R.S. Williams	DB4/862/L (Reg 92 LC 75)	4th Overall
14 April 1973	Hill Climb Wiscombe	R.S. Williams	DB4/862/L (Reg 92 LC 75)	1st in Class
14 April 1973	Hill Climb Wiscombe	A.J. House	DB4/GT/0124/R (Reg ELJ 5)	2nd in Class
14 April 1973	Hill Climb Wiscombe	G.M. Keane	DB4/GT/0157/R (Reg 41 DPX)	3rd in Class
14 April 1973	Hill Climb Wiscombe	K.L. Fuller	DB4/1149/R (Reg AMK 178 A)	4th in Class
14 April 1973	Hill Climb Wiscombe	P. Grant	DB4/833/R (Reg PJX 197)	5th in Class
14 April 1973	Hill Climb Wiscombe	C.L. Cottam	DB4/765/R (Reg 2385 PP)	7th in Class
14 April 1973	Hill Climb Wiscombe	Miss C. Clair	DB4/PP/108/R (Reg WLC 433)	9th in Class
15 April 1973	Climb of Champions	C.L. Cottam	DB4/765/R (Reg 2385 PP)	9th in Class

Date	Event	Driver	Chassis	Result
5 May 1973	Eight Clubs Meeting	R.S. Williams	DB4/862/L (Reg 92 LC 75)	6th Overall
3 June 1973	London M.C. Meeting	R.S. Williams	DB4/862/2 (Reg 92 LC 75)	2nd Overall
16 June 1973	AMOC Meeting	R.S. Williams	DB4/862/L (Reg 92 LC 75)	3rd in Class
16 June 1973	AMOC Meeting	N.R. Hamilton	DB4/0160/R (Reg 1 GRE)	4th in Class
16 June 1973	AMOC Meeting	K.L. Fuller	DB4/1149/R (Reg AMK 178 A)	4th in Class
16 June 1973	AMOC Meeting	Mrs. A Dent	DB4/820/L (Reg 3 BYR)	2nd in Class
16 June 1973	AMOC Meeting	Miss C. Clair	DB4/PP/108/R (Reg WLC 433)	3rd in Class
1 July 1973	Jaguar D.C. Hillclimb	R.S. Williams	DB4/862/L (Reg 92 LC 75)	2nd in Class
1 July 1973	Jaguar D.C. Hillclimb	M. Warren-Walker	DB4GT/0136/L (Reg 400 ABP)	3rd in Class
7 July 1973	AMOC Meeting	R.S. Williams	DB4/862/L (Reg 92 LC 75)	3rd in Class

Aston Martin DB4

Date	Event	Driver	Chassis	Result
7 July 1973	AMOC Meeting	N.R. Hamilton	DB4GT/0160/R (Reg 1 GRE)	6th Overall
22 July 1973	M.G.C.C. Meeting	I.H. Mason	DB4/239/R (Reg WLE 358)	13th Overall
29 July 1973	BRDC Meeting	R.S. Williams	DB4/862/L (Reg 92 LC 75)	4th Overall
12 August 1973	Halesowen M.C. Meeting	W.B. Fowler	DB4GT/0137/R (Reg BVD 115B)	4th in Class
25 August 1973	Bentley D.C. Meeting	N.R. Hamilton	DB4/0160/R (Reg 1 GRE)	4th Overall
15 September 1973	AMOC Meeting	N.R. Hamilton	DB4GT/0160/R (Reg 1 GRE)	4th Overall
16 September 1973	BARC Meeting	R.S. Williams	DB4/862/L (Reg 92 LC 75)	4th Overall
22 September 1973	Ferrari O.C. Meeting	R.S. Williams	DB4/862/L (Reg 92 LC 75)	1st Overall
27 October 1973	Nottingham S.C.C. Meeting	W.B. Fowler	DB4GT/0137/R (Reg BVD 115B)	4th in Class

Aston Martin DB4 Production Figures and Chassis Numbers

Model	Series	Production Date	Chassis Numbers
Aston Martin DB4	Series 1	October 1958 to February 1960	DB4/101 to DB4/250
Aston Martin DB4	Series 2	February 1960 to April 1961	DB4/251 to DB4/600
Aston Martin DB4	Series 3	April 1961 to September 1961	DB4/601 to DB4/765
Aston Martin DB4	Series 4	September 1961 to October 1962	DB4/766 to DB4/950
Aston Martin DB4	Series 5	September 1962 to June 1963	DB4/1001 to DB4 1050

A one-off Aston Martin DB4 GT by Bertone has the Chassis Number 0201/L and Engine Number 370/0201/GT.

It should be observed that Aston Martin DB4 Series 4 Vantage saloons used Chassis Numbers that ran from DB4/951 to DB4/995 whilst Aston Martin DB4 Series 5 Vantage saloons used Chassis Numbers that ran from DB4/1111 to DB4/1165 as well as DB4/1176 to DB4/1215.

Convertible Aston Martin DB4 Series 4 cars used Chassis Numbers DB4C/1051 to DB4C/1080 and Convertible Aston Martin DB4 Series 5 cars used Chassis Numbers DB4C/1081 to DB4C/1110 and DB4C/1166 to DB4C/1175.

Aston Martin DB4 Series 5 Convertible

Aston Martin DB4 Series 5 Convertible

Aston Martin DB4 Series 5 Convertible

Aston Martin DB5

The Aston Martin DB5 ran from July 1963 to September 1965. The Chassis Numbers ran from DB5C/1251 to DB5/2275.

Aston Martin DB5 Convertibles had Chassis Numbers of DB5C/1251 to 1300, DB5C/1501 to 1525, DB5C/1901 to 1925 and DB5C/2101 to 2123.

The number of Aston Martin DB5 Convertibles made was 123.

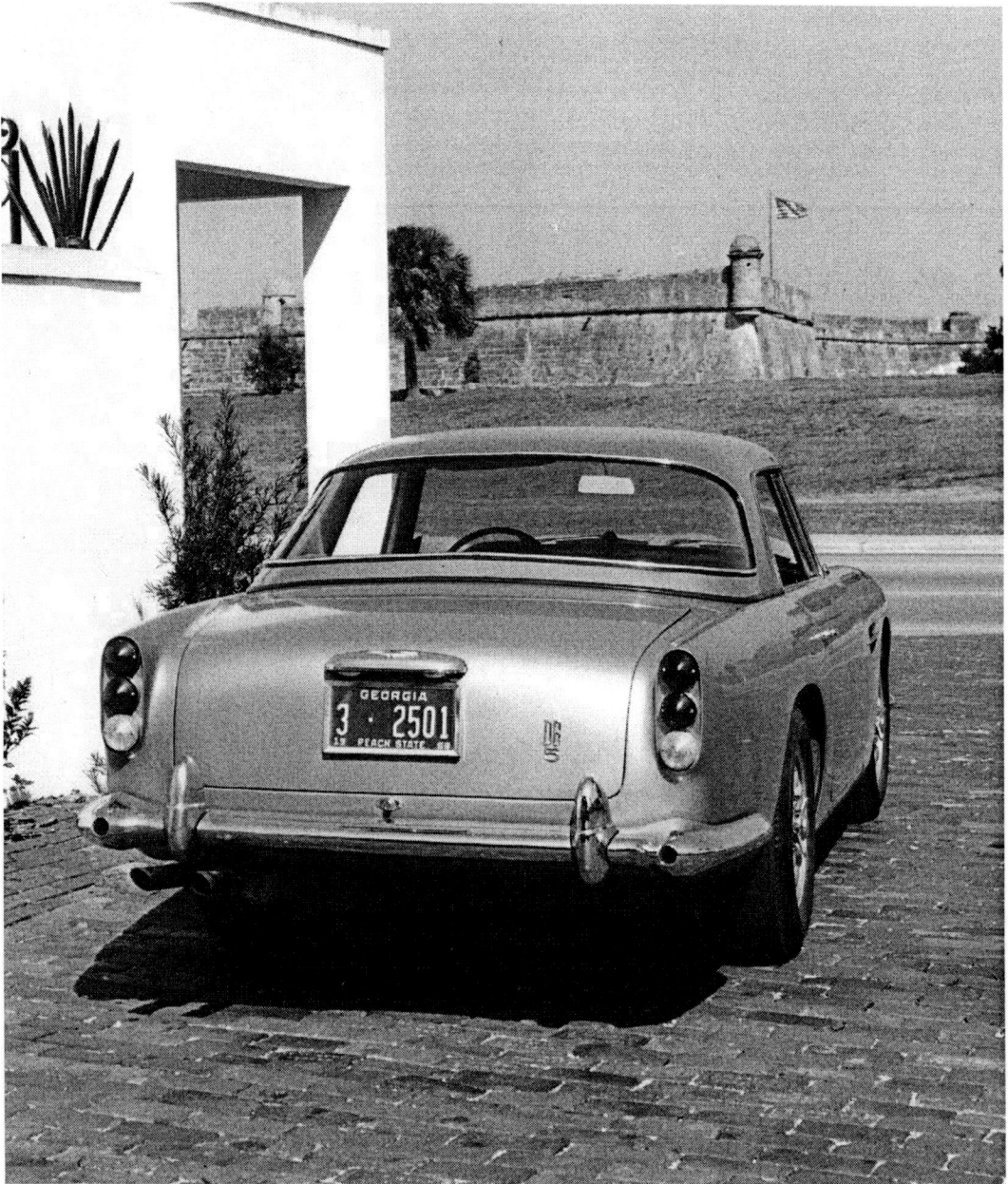

The Aston Martin DB5 had three 2 inch SU carburettors and developed 280 bhp at 5500 rpm.

The Aston Martin DB5 Vantage had three Weber 45mm DCOE carburettors and developed 310 bhp at 5500 rpm. This car became available in September 1964.

A small number of estate Aston Martin DB5s were made by Harold Radford. Twelve shooting brakes were made but used standard saloon chassis number (DB5C/1251 to DB5/2275).

Aston Martin DB5 Gallery

An Aston Martin DB5 being restored

The engine of this Aston Martin DB5 looks like new

Aston Martin DB5

Interior of this Aston Martin DB5 is undergoing restoration

Super engine bay of this Aston Martin DB5

Instruments and heating controls of the Aston Martin DB5

Tail lights of the Aston Martin DB5

A close-up of the Aston Martin DB5s engine bay

Still produced at Feltham, this DB5 has chassis number DB5/1450/R
and engine number 4001415

Rear tail light assembly of the Aston Martin DB5

Front headlamp of the Aston Martin DB5

Aston Martin DB5 Specifications

Engine

Cylinders:	6 in line
Bore:	96 mm (3.78 in.)
Stroke:	92 mm (3.62 in.)
Displacement::	3,995 cc (244 cu. in.)
Valve Gear:	Twin overhead camshafts
Compression Ratio:	8.9 to 1
Carburettors:	3 SU HD8
Fuel Pumps:	Twin SU electric
Oil Filter:	Full flow, renewable element
Maximum Power:	282 bhp (net) @ 5500 rpm
Maximum Torque:	280 lb. ft. @ 4500 rpm

Transmission

Clutch:	Laycock diaphragm spring, single dry plate, 10 in. diameter
Gearbox:	Five-speed, all-synchromesh,
Overall Ratios:	Top 0.83, Fourth 1.0, Third 1.23, Second 1.76, First 2.70, Reverse 3.31
Final drive:	Hypoid bevel, 3.77 to 1

Chassis

Construction:	Steel platform integral with tubular frame

Aston Martin DB5

Suspension

Front: Independent, wishbones and coil springs, telescopic dampers, anti-roll bar
Rear: live axle, trailing arms, coli springs, Watts linkage, Armstrong Selectaride adjustable lever-arm dampers
Steering: Rack and pinion
Wheel diameter: 16 in.

Brakes

Type: Girling disc front and rear with divided hydraulic circuits and twin vacuum servos
Dimensions: Front 11.5 in. diameter, Rear 10.8 in. diameter
Swept Area: Front 241 sq. in., Rear 197 sq. in. Total 438 sq. in. (269 sq. in. per ton laden)

Wheels

Type: Centre-lock, wire spokes, 5.5 in. wide rim
Tyres: 6.70 – 15 in. Avon Turbospeed with tubes

Equipment

Battery: 12-volt 60-amp. Hr.
Headlamps: Marchal 60-45 watt

Reversing lamps:	2, standard
Electric Fuses:	16 (including 2 spare)
Screen Wipers:	2-speed, self-parking
Screen Washer:	Standard, electric
Interior Heater:	Standard, fresh air
Safety Belts:	Extra, anchorages provided
Interior Trim:	Leather
Floor Covering:	Carpet
Starting Handle:	No provision
Jack:	Hydraulic, pillar-type
Jacking Points:	4, under body sills
Other Bodies:	Convertible and Hardtop
Fuel Tank:	19 imperial gallons (plus 3 gallon reserve)
Cooling System:	28 pints (including heater)
Engine Sump:	23 pints SAE 30. Change oil every 2500 miles; change filter element every 5000 miles
Gearbox:	3.5 pints SAE 90. Change oil every 10000 miles
Final Drive:	3 pints SAE 90. Change oil every 10000 miles
Grease:	9 points every 2,500 miles
Tyre Pressures:	Front 28; Rear 30 psi (normal driving). Front 35; Rear 40 psi (fast driving)

Performance Data

Top gear mph per 1000 rpm:	25.0
Mean piston speed at max. power:	3320 ft/min
Engine revs at mean max speed:	5650 rpm
BHP per ton laden	173

Fuel

Type:	Super Premium Grade (99.5 – 101 octane rating RM)
Estimated Consumption:	20.5 mpg (13.8 litres/100 km)
Normal Range:	12 – 21 mpg (13.2 – 23.5 litres/100 km)
Oil:	SAE 30. Consumption 1500 mpg

Fuel Consumption

At steady 30 mph:	26.0 mpg
40 mph:	26.5 mpg
50 mph:	25.3 mpg
60 mph:	24.2 mpg
70 mph:	22.5 mpg
80 mph:	21.1 mpg
90 mph:	19.8 mpg
100 mph:	17.6 mpg

Weight

Kerb Weight:	29.6 cwt (3310 lb, 1502 kg)
Front-Rear Distribution:	Front 50.8%, Rear 49.2%
Laden Weight:	32.6 cwt (3646 lb, 1653 kg)

Turning Circles

Between Kerbs:	Left 33 ft 11 inches, Right 36 ft 3 inches
Between Walls:	Left 36 ft 1 inch, Right 38 ft 5 inches
Turns lock-to-lock:	3.2

Aston Martin DB6

This photograph of Des O'Connor in the Aston Martin DB6 shows the revised seats which improved comfort, while other changes on the Aston Martin DB6 included a slightly more steeply raked windscreen.

Additionally, it was during the Aston Martin DB5s life that manufacturing facilities were all brought under one roof at Newport Pagnell. The Aston Martin DB5 was the last car from the Feltham factory and by the time of the Aston Martin DB6 everything was at Newport Pagnell. The Aston Martin DB6 was announced in October 1965. Similar to the Aston Martin DB5 at the front, but it had a divided front bumper.

Aston Martin DB6 Vantage

The DB6 Mark II Vantage engine had triple 45DCOE Weber carburettors

In Vantage form it had a compression ratio of 9.4 to 1

The Vantage engine option was available on the Aston Martin DB6
Mark II

Engine bay of the Aston Martin DB6 Mark II Vantage

Improved dashboard of the Aston Martin DB6 was used in both Volante and closed versions of the car. This is the Volante version

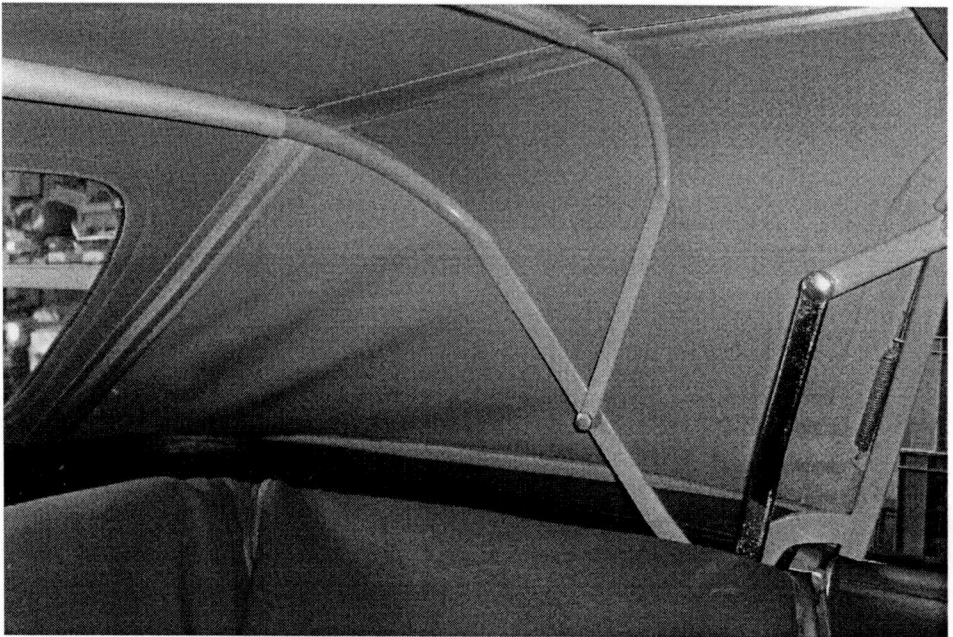

The hood of the Aston Martin DB6 Volante

Aston Martin DB6

The Aston Martin DB6 Mark I that was produced from October 1965 to July 1969 had Chassis Numbers that ran from DB6/2351/R to DB6/3599/LC.

The Aston Martin DB6 Mark II that was produced from July 1969 to November 1970 and had more flared wheel arches was given Chassis Numbers that ran from DB6MK2/4101/R to DB6MK2/4345/R.

The Aston Martin DB6 Volante Mark I had Chassis Numbers DBVC/3600/R to DBVC/3739/R. It was made between October 1966 and July 1969, with 140 being built.

The Aston Martin DB6 Volante Mark II had Chassis Numbers from DB6MK2VC/3751/R to DB6MK2VC/3788/L. Only 38 were made.

Aston Martin DB6 Specifications and Performance

Engine:	6 Cylinder
Bore and Stroke:	96 mm x 92 mm
Displacement:	3,995 cc
Compression Ratio:	8.9 to 1
Carburettors:	Weber 45 DCO
Maximum Power:	325 bhp @ 5750 rpm
Maximum Torque:	290 lb ft @ 4500 rpm

Gear Ratios:

Top	0.83
Fourth	1.00
Third	1.23
Second	1.76
First	2.70
Reverse	3.31

Front Suspension:	Independent, wishbones, coil springs, anti-roll bar, telescopic dampers
Rear Suspension:	Live axle, trailing arms, coil springs, Watts linkage, Armstrong Selectaride lever-arm dampers
0-60 mph:	6.5 seconds
30-70 mph:	5.6 seconds through the gears
Maximum Speed:	148 mph

Aston Martin DB6 Competition Car

Aston Martin DB6 Competition Car in the workshop

The car of Adrian "Gus" Pope and Julian Reddyhough was entry number 76 in the Liege Rome Liege Rally

Aston Martin DB6

Interior of a Competition Aston Martin DB6

Aston Martin DB6

Engine bay of the Aston Martin DB6 Competition Car

Aston Martin DB6

Special seats on this Aston Martin DB6

Passenger side of the Aston Martin DB6 Competition Car

Aston Martin DB4, DB5 and DB6 Production Figures

Aston Martin DB4 Series 1	150 cars
Aston Martin DB4 Series 2	350 cars
Aston Martin DB4 Series 3	165 cars
Aston Martin DB4 Series 4	230 cars
Aston Martin DB4 Series 4 convertible	30 cars
Aston Martin DB4 Series 5	145 cars
Aston Martin DB4 Series 5 convertible	40 cars
Aston Martin DB4 GT	75 cars
Aston Martin DB4 GT Zagato	19 cars
Aston Martin DB4 GT Bertone	1 car
Aston Martin DB5	898 cars
Aston Martin DB5 convertible	123 cars
Aston Martin Volante SWB	37 cars
Aston Martin DB6	1327 cars
Aston Martin DB6 Mk II	240 cars
Aston Martin Volante Mk I	140 cars
Aston Martin Volante Mk II	38 cars

Aston Martin DB5 and DB6

Two views of the Aston Martin DB6 and Volante

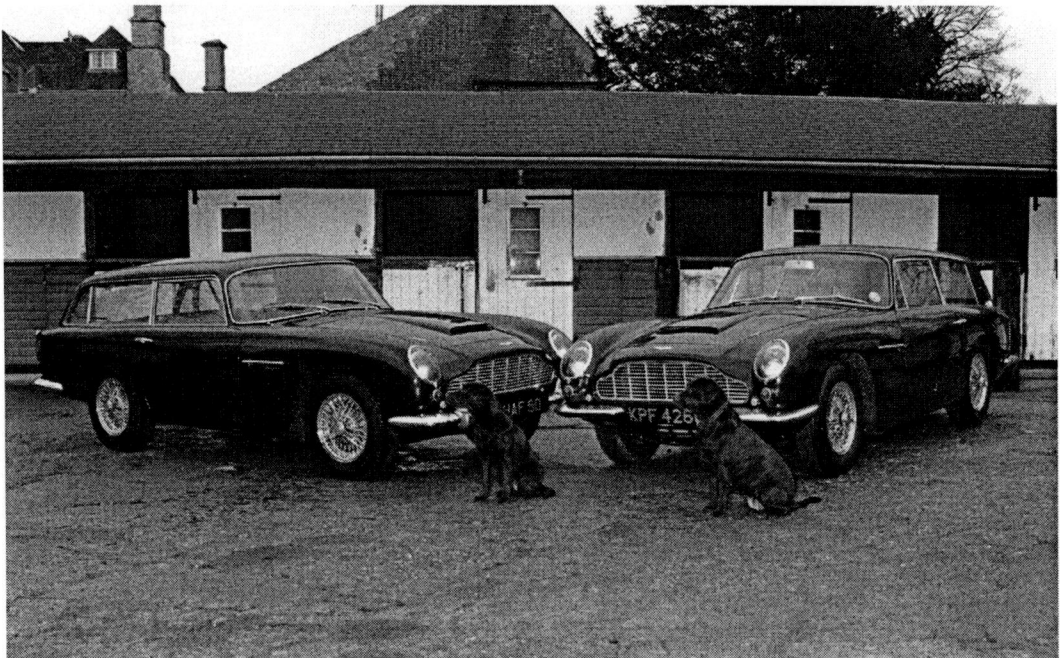

Aston Martin DB5 and DB6 estate cars

Aston Martin Owners Clubs

Aston Martin Owners Club
(Switzerland)

Jürg Furter (President)
Eglistrasse 2
CH-8942 Oberrieden
SWITZERLAND

Aston Martin Owners Club
(Germany)

Bernd-Heinrich Schriever
Platanenallee 16
22529 Hamburg
GERMANY

Aston Martin Owners Club
(Australia)

Dr. Jason Vochala
4th Floor
124 Exhibition Street
Melbourne 3000
AUSTRALIA

Aston Martin Owners Club
(Sweden)

Thomas Hedberg
Stomvägen 21B
428 30 Källered
SWEDEN

Aston Martin Owners Club of
Western Australia

Mr. Jim Tweddle
PO Box 1260
Booragoon
Western Australia 6153
AUSTRALIA

Aston Martin Owners Club
(America)

Mr. Larry Davis
6578 Crystalaire Drive
San Diego
CA 92120-3951
USA